Cambridge Elements

Elements in Music and the City
Simon McVeigh
University of London
Abigail Wood
University of Haifa

LIBERATION ON THE DANCE FLOOR

Popular Music and the Promise of Plurality

Craig Jennex
Toronto Metropolitan University

Shaftesbury Road, Cambridge CB2 8EA, United Kingdom

One Liberty Plaza, 20th Floor, New York, NY 10006, USA

477 Williamstown Road, Port Melbourne, VIC 3207, Australia

314–321, 3rd Floor, Plot 3, Splendor Forum, Jasola District Centre, New Delhi – 110025, India

103 Penang Road, #05–06/07, Visioncrest Commercial, Singapore 238467

Cambridge University Press is part of Cambridge University Press & Assessment, a department of the University of Cambridge.

We share the University's mission to contribute to society through the pursuit of education, learning and research at the highest international levels of excellence.

www.cambridge.org
Information on this title: www.cambridge.org/9781009507615
DOI: 10.1017/9781009351812

© Craig Jennex 2025

This publication is in copyright. Subject to statutory exception and to the provisions of relevant collective licensing agreements, with the exception of the Creative Commons version the link for which is provided below, no reproduction of any part may take place without the written permission of Cambridge University Press & Assessment.

An online version of this work is published at doi.org/10.1017/9781009351812 under a Creative Commons Open Access license CC-BY-NC 4.0 which permits re-use, distribution and reproduction in any medium for non-commercial purposes providing appropriate credit to the original work is given and any changes made are indicated. To view a copy of this license visit https://creativecommons.org/licenses/by-nc/4.0

When citing this work, please include a reference to the DOI 10.1017/9781009351812

First published 2025

A catalogue record for this publication is available from the British Library

ISBN 978-1-009-50761-5 Hardback
ISBN 978-1-009-35180-5 Paperback
ISSN 2633-3880 (online)
ISSN 2633-3872 (print)

Cambridge University Press & Assessment has no responsibility for the persistence or accuracy of URLs for external or third-party internet websites referred to in this publication and does not guarantee that any content on such websites is, or will remain, accurate or appropriate.

For EU product safety concerns, contact us at Calle de José Abascal, 56, 1°, 28003 Madrid, Spain, or email eugpsr@cambridge.org

Liberation on the Dance Floor

Popular Music and the Promise of Plurality

Elements in Music and the City

DOI: 10.1017/9781009351812
First published online: August 2025

Craig Jennex
Toronto Metropolitan University

Author for correspondence: Craig Jennex, craigjennex@torontomu.ca

Abstract: Lesbian and gay liberation movements of the twentieth century were made possible through heterogeneous dance music cultures that flourished in urban spaces. In an era of profound political challenges, collective dance enabled lesbian and gay individuals to connect with their bodies and the bodies of others, experience a sense of communal belonging, explore non-normative gender and sexual desires, and perceive individual and collective power in a heteronormative reality that regularly suppressed both. For lesbians and gays, collective dance introduced them to difference as a dynamic catalyst of political change, allowing them to experience the promise of liberation. This Element combines ethnographic research, archival materials, and popular music histories to analyze the role of popular music participation in lesbian and gay liberation in US cities and demonstrate how collective dance served as a transformative site of political contestation and imagination. This title is also available as Open Access on Cambridge Core.

Keywords: lesbian and gay liberation, popular music, collective dance, LGBTQ2+ history, queer politics

© Craig Jennex 2025

ISBNs: 9781009507615 (HB), 9781009351805 (PB), 9781009351812 (OC)
ISSNs: 2633-3880 (online), 2633-3872 (print)

Contents

	Preface	1
1	Introduction: The Political Force of Collective Dance	3
2	Dance and Resistance	15
3	Dancing to Liberation	29
4	Collective Heat	41
5	Disease on the Dance Floor	49
6	Conclusion: We Should Be Dancing	61
	References	66

Preface

We should be dancing. I begin with this simple statement because it captures both the thesis of this Element and the broader longing that informs my research on music participation in queer pasts, presents, and futures. For me, queerness is best understood as a form of unbound and extraordinary relationality – a way of being with others in embodied, erotic, and hopeful ways. Queerness is a promise: that something better is possible; that we are not limited to the normative logics of the moment; and that we can be together, across forms of difference, in ways that are mutually beneficial and breathtakingly beautiful. The best dance floor experiences can model precisely this type of togetherness and can thus serve as a blueprint for queer relationality that might serve us well elsewhere. When we give ourselves fully to the sound of dance music, the promise of queerness, and the recognition of our sharedness – our necessary plurality – we can access feelings that are largely unattainable elsewhere in a world structured by heteronormativity. I'm not being hyperbolic; we should be dancing.

On the dance floor our bodies are distinct, but we are bound together through our corporeal orientation to the same musical sound and our adherence to its temporal structures. Surrounded by others and out of time together, we can connect with ourselves, each other, and the possibility of collective bliss. As we find one another on the dance floor we also find a shared recognition that this experience is outside of the tedious, demoralizing logics that govern our everyday. Here, so much of what constrains our behaviors and fantasies can fall away. In this moment, our attention is not focused on what currently is, but instead on what could be. Together we catch a glimpse of the potential of something better. We are overwhelmed with a sense of feeling good – feeling *really good* – and in this moment anything seems possible.

I hope you have experienced something similar to the feelings I am describing. I have a few times, though for me such experiences are not guaranteed. When I do access this sense of overwhelming and erotically charged bliss, it is always fleeting; it usually lasts a few bars, maybe a full musical phrase if I'm lucky. But it always slips away, no matter how tightly I try to hold on to it. Although the feelings fade, their aftermath is long-lasting. Dance floor bliss is performative in the sense that it has a series of effects. One effect is that tapping into these feelings can radically reshape my understanding of the world. If you have yet to experience the feelings I'm describing here, I hope you can imagine them. The mere possibility of collective bliss can serve as a beacon that gives us something to work toward while simultaneously illuminating the place where we currently stand – this place that, while not enough, can be reanimated by a shared desire for something more.

My argument in *Liberation on the Dance Floor* is that dance experiences during the lesbian and gay liberation era created the conditions for people to perceive collective liberation as both possible and worthwhile. The dances I describe in this Element are not secondary to or less significant than those acts we tend to historicize as legitimately political – protests, marches, legislative and judicial battles, and the like. As I will show, collective dance is a transformative political act in its own right. And it's one that is too often overlooked when conceiving of ways that people have changed – and can change – the world. What I'm describing throughout this Element is the political force of a utopian possibility that is embodied in collective music participation and in histories of queer collective formation. In the spirit of the dance floor, this Element longs for and surrenders to moments of convergence and collectivity that challenge our understanding of self and other – of what was, what is, and what could be. It represents a longing for a future that is only made possible by pasts that are messy, transient, sweaty, and partially inscrutable from a contemporary perspective. These future-based desires – whether they are perceptible in the past or the present – are worth straining our ears to hear and our bodies to experience.

The types of collective social dance that I explore in this Element allow participants to embrace their body, the bodies of others, and the broader possibility of a political, collective body. They encourage a sense of temporal presentness – of being in the here and now – by demarcating affective experiences of time and space outside the ordinary structures of everyday. They derive meaning from the fact that they are at once singular and plural, both profoundly intimate and necessarily shared, and have the capacity to materialize previously unimaginable avenues for individual and collective ways of being. Throughout the writing of this Element, I was fortunate to spend time with archival materials, recorded music, and personal memories shared through ethnographic interviews that made the profound potential of collective dance clear. Collective dance is no minor aspect of queer history in North America; it *is* queer history. And as I argue throughout this Element, it must be queer future too.

At some point while writing, I came to realize that this Element is not just about a history of lesbian and gay dance experiences, but also about the process and promise of falling in love – stupidly, uncontrollably, wholeheartedly – through shared participation in musical sound. On the dance floor, participants fall in love with others, with ideas, and with the promise that something else is possible and worth fighting for. In this Element, I attempt to describe experiences that are simultaneously enigmatic and overwhelming – those brief moments in life when everything you know is upended. For some people, what I'm describing here might be closer to their understanding of "lust" than "love." That's fair. I'm impressed that you can parse the two concepts; I've never been able to tell the difference. What I am interested in are those moments of overwhelming and impassioned desire when we feel swept up in something that is momentarily immortal, bursting with promise, and fully embodied. It doesn't matter if these feelings are permanent; what matters is that they enable us to envision and do things we had not previously considered possible. Whatever we might call these overwhelming feelings of desire, they carry with them the capacity to radically reshape one's life and purpose. There is promise in that potentiality – of balancing on the threshold of bliss that is also a threshold of agony – and in shared recognition of how the extraordinary can change our relationship to the ordinary.

While the histories I unpack in this Element are real and performative, the structures and promises of feelings I describe might be a little harder for some readers to recognize and believe in. My commitment to an unspecified queerer future – an opaque potential with vague contours that we should strive for together – asks a lot of you as a reader. But I hope you'll join me on the dance floor and in this search for signs of collective bliss across time. We should take the leap. We should be dancing.

1 Introduction: The Political Force of Collective Dance

> I suspect that for some politicos—straight or queer—the association of dancing and revolution is evidence of just how trivial gay liberation is. But, if so, they don't know much about history.
>
> — John D'Emilio, "Let's Dance!"

In this Element, I situate social dance and popular music participation as fundamental to lesbian and gay liberation movements in Canadian and American cities from the late 1960s to the late 1980s. Collective dance in this era enabled lesbian and gay individuals to feel their bodies and the bodies of others, experience a sense of belonging, explore their nonnormative gender and sexual desires, and perceive individual and collective power in a heteronormative reality built on suppressing both. For many lesbian and gay individuals in this historical period, collective dance was the means through which they were introduced to feelings of how good queerness could feel and the alluring promise of collective liberation. During an era marked by profound harm through homophobic violence at the hands of fellow citizens and the police, the AIDS epidemic,[1] moralistic representations of gay life, and government agencies that were dismissive of or explicitly hostile to queer life, collective

---

[1] Throughout this Element, I refer to AIDS and the AIDS epidemic to reflect the historical discourse of the 1980s, when HIV had not yet been identified as the virus that, over time, can cause AIDS. Contemporary discourse tends to emphasize HIV/AIDS as a term that also includes people living with HIV.

dance to popular music allowed lesbian and gay individuals to perceive the promise and possibility of something better.

Sylvester, the brilliant San Francisco-based disco diva, famously sang that the dance floor can make us "feel mighty real." On the surface, Sylvester's lyrical address might seem a bit precious, but a generous reading of his falsetto fantasies puts him in conversation with pathbreaking scholarship published decades later. In her book *Moving Politics*, Deborah B. Gould (2009, p. 3) argues that "feeling and emotion are fundamental to political life" as "there is an affective dimension to the processes and practices that make up 'the political,' broadly defined." Before political desires can be articulated in words, Gould argues, they must be felt, experienced, perceived in bodies. Affect is a primary force of political change for Gould (2009, p. 27) precisely because feelings "can shake one out of deeply grooved patterns of thinking ... and allow for new imaginings." Following Gould's lead, I ask: how did collective dance play a role in the development of the affective states and political horizons of lesbian and gay liberation movements? How did collective participation in popular music alter the contours of what participants sensed as possible, desirable, and necessary?

Throughout this Element, I frequently employ the term "dance music" as a way of signaling that music heard on dance floors often refuses and challenges easy categorization. As Tim Lawrence (2022, pp. 307–8) notes, the commonplace usage of "disco" to describe dance music of the 1970s belies the fact that "the genre didn't exist until the decade was almost halfway over" and that "whatever came before didn't sound like straight-up disco and didn't acquire or need a single name." Whatever we call the dance music that soundtracks queer histories of the twentieth century – soul, R&B, funk, disco, dance, house, garage, ballroom, or others – they are bound together by their indebtedness to Black musical genealogies (even when diluted versions of the genres are taken up in the white mainstream) and a fundamental reversal of musical sensibilities that might seem unfamiliar for people accustomed to white, Western musical traditions that emphasize complexities of pitch in melody and harmony. Anthony Thomas (1989, p. 29) argues this in relation to house music, warning, "don't dismiss the simple chord changes, the echoing percussion lines, and the minimalist melody: in African music the repetition of well-chosen rhythms is crucial to the dynamic of the music." John Chernoff (1979, pp. 111–12) agrees and emphasizes the importance of repetitive rhythms as central to experiencing African- and African American–influenced dance music, arguing that "repetition of a well-chosen rhythm continually re-affirms the power of the music by locking that rhythm, and the people listening or dancing to it, into a dynamic and open structure." As will become clear: lesbian and gay political histories are built on a sense of collective queer possibility that was actualized through participation in Black musical traditions. From the late 1960s on, individuals committed to the ideals of lesbian and gay liberation envisioned and felt collective political possibility to the sound of music that was, more often than not, first rendered audible in gay Black dance spaces.

Urban-based dance floors across North America – particularly those operated by lesbian and gay community groups in the 1970s and 1980s – allowed lesbian and gay people to sense the possibility of liberation and to experience embodied queer desires through the sounds of pulsating dance music (see Figure 1). My framing of the mid 1960s to the mid 1980s as a discernible era of lesbian and gay political formation is an attempt to bind the years leading up to the Stonewall Riots in New York City to the early years of the AIDS epidemic when neoliberal political ideologies, economic policies, and modes of governance worked to defang collective political movements that seemed primed to radically reshape American and Canadian societies.

While queer dance floor experiences offered a sense of relief from the realities of heteronormative patriarchy, it would be incorrect to interpret such moments as mere escapism. The experiences that I take up in this Element allowed people to feel the possibility of a safer, queerer, more collective world. Being attuned to and subsequently working toward the possibility of something better is a

Figure 1 Dance at the Gay Activists Alliance Firehouse in New York City, 1971. Manuscript and Archives Division, The New York Public Library. Photograph by Diana Davies.

transformative form of engagement with the inadequate present. In other words, these brief moments of bliss are dance floor performatives: they materialize the possibility of something better. Such moments are somewhat difficult to capture and describe, however, because they are inherently fleeting. For some individuals, these feelings may be stimulated by alcohol or narcotics, making them even more difficult to articulate and unpack. But the ephemerality of these moments is not a detriment. Instead, it is part of what makes experiencing these feelings so moving and revelatory: they exist outside of normative, everyday time and provide an alternative vision of the life one might live. If these feelings were attainable all the time or easily accessible, they would be less alluring.

I am interested in understanding these dance floor spaces and the experiences therein as allowing participants to access feelings of bliss and the promise of collective potential. My approach is heavily influenced by José Esteban Muñoz's (2009, p. 1) *Cruising Utopia: The Then and There of Queer Futurity*, particularly his argument that queerness is "essentially about the rejection of a here and now and an insistence on potentiality or concrete possibility for another world." My thinking is also informed by the work of Jill Dolan (2010, p. 2), whose book *Utopia in Performance: Finding Hope at the Theatre* analyzes brief but enchantingly transformative moments in live performance through which "audiences feel themselves allied with each other, and with a broader, more capacious sense of public, in which social discourse articulates the possible, rather than the insurmountable obstacles to human potential." Building on the work of these scholars, as well as on firsthand accounts from interviews I conducted with activists, DJs, dancers, and organizers involved in the lesbian and gay liberation movement, I argue that experiences on dance floors of this era encouraged feelings of bliss and belonging that had the capacity to change one's perspectives on the world and their capacities within it. For many of the individuals I interviewed, dancing with other people marked as deviant simultaneously allowed them to feel like they were part of something larger and that a different reality was worth fighting for. The specific details of what a better world might look like are largely unimportant to me in this Element; I am interested instead in the powerful feelings attainable on the dance floor that make a queerer world seem possible.

While I perceive collective dance as a dynamic and productive means of radical imagination and political change, I am not suggesting that any of the dance floors I explore in this Element are actualized sites of utopia. Indeed, many dance music spaces popular during the lesbian and gay liberation era were managed in ways that reflected the normative ideologies and discriminatory hierarchies of the time. Luis Manuel Garcia-Mispireta (2023, p. 1) reminds us that dance floors "are places where both inclusion and exclusion happen" and that the sense of "strategic vagueness" that often binds dancers together enables them to "temporarily enjoy a moment of belonging unburdened by the difficult work of 'identity politics,' while at the same time enabling them to ignore the exclusions and injustices taking place on those same dancefloors." Several dance venues in the 1970s and 1980s, for example, utilized by-invitation-only door policies to actively exclude individuals on the basis of race, class, and gender. As Lawrence (2004, p. 79) notes, some bars – including, famously, The Tenth Floor, which opened in New York City in 1972 – used discriminatory door policies to keep their dance floors "overwhelmingly Caucasian." While the predominant whiteness was reflected by the patrons, the entire concept of the venue – from the music being played to the styles of dance embraced – relied on genealogies of African American and Latinx social cultures. White supremacy was not the only broader social ideology that animated dance spaces in these decades. As Alice Echols (2010, p. 77) argues, changes in regulations and social permissibility in the 1970s meant that "women, who had for years operated as dance floor beards (that is, as heterosexualizing covers) for gay men, were suddenly expendable, and often unwelcome" in the new, gay male–oriented dance venues. The gendered realities of dance floors during this era were not only skewed by active, intentional exclusion; under patriarchy, women were less likely to have disposable income than men and were also less likely to have access to public urban spaces. In an interview published in *Out of the Closets: Voices of Gay Liberation*, Marsha P. Johnson (1992, p. 114) describes "unfriendly" Gay Activist Alliance (GAA) dances in New York City: "[w]e still feel oppression by other gay brothers. Gay sisters don't think too bad of transvestites. Gay brothers do. I went to a dance at Gay Activists Alliance just last week ... those men weren't too friendly at all." For Johnson, the reception she received at GAA dances stemmed from systems of gender classification and racial hierarchies that inform our social worlds – even those social worlds that claim radical or alternative understandings of sexuality.

To be sure, participating in homosexual acts does not mean that a person is innately resistant to stultifying or oppressive cultural logics. The same is true for spaces that invite or enable queer connectivity: gender, class, and racial hierarchies are not necessarily challenged by the sound of throbbing dance music and erotic homosexual contact. Louis Niebur (2022, pp. 2–3) offers an example of this in his book *Menergy*, writing that while most white gay men who danced to disco in San Francisco's Castro district remember a "utopian environment where all individuals were welcomed equally," the people of color he interviewed "without exception ... recalled incident after incident of racist behaviour, both institutionally and by individuals in the Castro." Longing for lesbian and gay liberation does not necessarily mean recognizing the importance of other forms of liberation;

indeed, as Audre Lorde (1984, p. 116) makes clear, it might make the political importance of related battles even harder to discern. Lorde concisely summarizes this practice, arguing that "those of us who stand outside [the trappings of] power often identify one way in which we are different, and we assume that to be the primary cause of all oppression, forgetting other distortions around difference, some of which we ourselves may be practicing." Tensions of and anxieties around differences of identity, political goals, and methods permeated dance experiences in the 1970s and 1980s. Such internal struggles were seldom easy to navigate, but they were vital to the formation of political collectivity and the imaginative capacities provoked by dance floor participation. Instances where heterogeneous queer collectives convened across difference in embodied and affective ways radically reshaped North American cities in the lesbian and gay liberation era.

As interviews with dancers, DJs, and other activists of the era make clear, dances were perceived as welcoming and accessible to individuals who considered themselves not adequately political. This adds another complication to excavating this history, as many of the people with whom I spoke – whose actions and desires fundamentally shaped the world in which we now live – do not consider their work "real" activism. One DJ I spoke with, immediately after explaining that they would take song requests at early lesbian and gay dances in Toronto so that "everyone felt they had a say in the night and the communal experience," later added, "but I was never an *activist* activist." The histories I explore in this Element are full of trailblazing activists who refuse the label and downplay the importance of their work at every turn. Several people I spoke with referenced other, "real activists" who were "doing the real work" – comments that are not only informed by individual humility but also by the broader social interpretation of carnal pleasures as antithetical to proper politics.

F. Enke (2007, p. 7) reminds us that participants in a political movement bring along their various interests and, indeed, some steadfastly refuse association with the movement. They argue that many of the individuals who did vital feminist work "did not even consider themselves activists. Many softball players, for example, said they wanted above all to play ball; it happened that doing so required challenging the gender-, sexual-, class-, and race-based arrangements of civic space." In other words: activism often exceeds identification with political movements. This isn't necessarily detrimental. bell hooks (1984, p. 30) pointed out long ago that "emphasis on identity ... is appealing because it creates a false sense that one is engaged in praxis." In the same way that claiming queer identity doesn't necessarily mean a person is engaged in queer politics, refusing the label of activist doesn't mean that a person's work isn't activism, or that the interpretive lens of activism can't allow us to better understand a person's political engagements.

Because dances were perceived as easier to attend than explicitly activist events, and because they engendered feelings of collaborative agency, collective dance regularly served as an entry into a political community as the contours of that community were forming, shifting, and expanding. However, collective dance did not simply allow people access to an already existing community; rather, dance floor collectives formed and reformed meaningful connections imbued with thrilling feelings of belonging, plurality, and eroticism. While always productive, the alternatives sparked by nonnormative social and collective behaviors are particularly promising under homophobic logic that attempts to contain queer bodies, desires, and behaviors.

While my primary focus in this Element is on the hopeful feelings that collective dance encourages, I am also concerned with the material and financial effects of popular music and dance experiences. Dances, perhaps more than any other collective endeavor, funded lesbian and gay liberation in North American cities during the 1970s and 1980s. While money raised through dance parties was essential to launch organizations in the early years of lesbian and gay liberation, it continued to be important in the 1980s – a decade of neoliberal reorganization that emphasized individual responsibility, saw the privatization of public goods and services, and valued interpersonal competition over collective good. Within this brutal reality, communal social endeavors that provided financial support for forms of resistance to the social order and enabled a sense of collectivity were both difficult and increasingly necessary.

The dance cultures that I attend to here are far more important to broader lesbian and gay liberation movements than we might imagine – and certainly more significant than most historicizing of the era suggests. If the practice of collective dance surfaces at all in the historical record of lesbian and gay liberation in North American cities, it is often presented as an enjoyable reprieve from the brutal heteronormative reality of the moment, but tangential to the so-called real activism of the movements. As Niebur (2022, p. 11) notes, "while rarely identified as 'political' spaces, the discos and bars of the 1970s were among the first public places where many celebrated their status as out gay men." The dismissal of dance spaces and the cleaving of pleasure and politics are partly a result of contemporary thinking that suggests "proper" political progress for marginalized populations comes from individualistic legal and legislative battles. While I recognize and celebrate individuals whose conflicts with the state through judicial avenues have dramatically reshaped the trajectory of the lives of younger LGBTQ2+ people, I am interested in tracing the messier narratives of dynamic historical queer collectives that are produced through musical sound and experiences in which we can, as Sylvester suggests, feel mighty real.

There are several reasons why I am drawn to these affective musical collectives over narratives of individual heroism in relation to the state. First, convening with others through dance music can radicalize a participant and reify their unconventional desires in pleasurable and creative ways. Second, the ephemeral yet profound affiliations forged on the dance floor provide a model for queer politics and sociality that moves away from the simplicity of rigid identification. Third, an individualistic perspective on LGBTQ2+ history overlooks crucial collective endeavors that shaped social movements and propelled political change. And, finally, framing progressive politics as requiring benevolence from governmental bodies strikes me as shortsighted. As David Eng (2010, p. 4) compellingly shows, the state as savior and site of redemption only seems logical for certain LGBTQ2+ subjects privileged in a myriad of other ways and is predicated on the systematic "dissociation of (homo) sexuality from race as coeval and intersecting phenomena." Queerness is a form of innovation; it is most compelling when it turns away from what is already established.

Queerness is most promising when it is embodied, collective, and expanding – when it signals something not yet here, but something worth reaching for and moving toward. This is why dance floor collectivity is so important both in a broad sense – in creating queer possibility within a social world that is conditioned by cis- and heteronormativity – and within LGBTQ2+ communities that often mimic the very exclusions we repudiate in broader society. There is a promise of the queer dance floor that we must orient ourselves toward, even if we never quite reach that promise. As Frances Negron-Muntaner (2011, p. 311) reminds us, "dance is never just dancing; it is a medium for identity and a fulcrum for political mobilization." What happens on the dance floor is political work with moments of friction and discomfort where contrasting desires are worked out and worked through. For musicologist Barry Shank (2014), the process of navigating conflicting understandings of the present, past, and future through experiences of musical beauty is one way a collective enters the register of the political.

In the classic anthology *Lavender Culture*, Rob Dobson (1979, p. 171) writes, "For me, dance is one of the tools for 'stopping the world,' for helping me to enter the eternal present, letting each moment be fresh and new, exploring the infinite universe, making endless discoveries, untainted by anything I've ever been told about the nature of things." This idea was repeated by many of the people I spoke with for this Element: surrendering oneself to music and dance can elicit transformative feelings and potentialize new ways of being. Such experiences in the lesbian and gay era, and the possibilities that reverberate in their wake, teach us a great deal about what could be – both what was once imagined as possible and what we might use to fuel our imagination in the present. The past is rife with musical pleasures and fleeting visions of better futures that have long been overlooked as sites of political agency and transformation. We should return to these historical moments and let that music once again enliven our bodies and connections with one another – not just to better understand these pasts, but to embrace and embody the logic of liberation in the present. To return to Dobson's (1979, p. 172) chapter in *Lavender Culture*: "I won't really be satisfied until I see everyone in the world dancing. But I might settle for just a few other faggots to share it with."

1.1 Homosexual Panic

In most North American cities in the mid twentieth century, dancing with a person of the same sex was practically – and in some cases explicitly – prohibited. In the eyes of respectable citizens, police, politicians, and religious leaders, same-sex social dance was vulgar and dangerous. As an overt and public manifestation of illicit sexual desires and gender behaviors, homosexuals convening on a dance floor and moving their bodies to music was perceived by many people in positions of authority as a threat to acceptable forms of morality and, ultimately, a threat to the proper functioning of society.

Following the disruption of the Second World War – including the mobilization of soldiers on the warfront and laborers at home – the vast majority of North Americans were keen to return to an idealized normalcy in which ostensibly happy heterosexual families served as the building blocks of their nations. A widespread reinvestment in and glorification of heteronormative patriarchy after the war was also a response to the way gender-segregated spaces of warfare fomented previously undiscovered queer possibilities. Paul Jackson (2004, p. 17) argues that "the war was a time of sexual self-discovery" for many young people who found freedom away from their hometowns and the watchful eyes of family and friends. For many young people coming of age during the Second World War, the disruption to their conventional life trajectory alongside the intimate bonds they made with others during wartime potentialized queer desires and behaviors. John D'Emilio (1983, p. 24) argues that the Second World War "created a substantially new 'erotic situation' conducive both to the articulation of a homosexual identity and to the more rapid evolution of a gay subculture." The budding possibility of queerness provoked by the cultural shifts in the wake of the war was widely seen as a remnant of a disruptive and painful time that many wanted to leave in the past. Collective same-sex social dancing was particularly galling in this context, as groups of deviants gathered and flaunted their perverse lifestyle in embodied, erotic, and joyful ways.

In the years after the Second World War, both Canada and the United States experienced economic booms that enabled a different way of living for many of the nations' citizens: leisure time and disposable income increased, and affluent white families moved out of cities' downtown areas to chase the American Dream in newly constructed suburban developments. While the shifting realities of cities across North America are locally distinct, there are broad trends that set the stage for the development of lesbian and gay subcultures in urban spaces in the 1960s and 1970s. Many downtowns in cities across the continent emptied out and buildings in certain parts of urban spaces were abandoned. The deterioration of downtown communities resulted in cheaper rents that enabled the development of spaces for marginalized collectives – including spaces that would bring together gays and lesbians. The postwar development of urban spaces in many North American cities provided more anonymity to individuals who enjoyed queer desires than suburbs and small towns might have allowed. At the same time, the development of urban apartment buildings allowed for single and shared nonfamily occupancy. Taken together, shifts in demographics and organization of urban spaces enabled the formation of collective queer life in spaces that had only recently been populated by heterosexual families.

General awareness of homosexuality increased in North America in the decades after the Second World War. Visible homosexual subcultures developed in cities and received significant and sensationalized attention from the tabloid press; popular novels that incorporate nonnormative desires, experiences, and themes introduced homosexuality to mainstream literary audiences; and claims made by Alfred Kinsey and other sexologists turned homosexuality into a talking point throughout the United States and Canada, sparked by the shocking claims that significantly more people had participated in or desired same-sex erotic experiences than one might imagine and that it's not always possible to identify a homosexual simply by looking at them. These social changes coincided with structural shifts that refined homosexual behaviors into homosexual identities: the aforementioned increase in disposable income and construction of multiunit apartment and condominium buildings meant that people (especially men) with queer desires could move away from the demands of the heteronormative family structure and live a "gay life" in the big city.

While the possibility of life structured around homosexual identity was exciting for some, it was perceived by others to be catastrophic. At the federal level, both the United States and Canada developed campaigns against homosexuals in the Armed Forces and civil service. David K. Johnson (2004, p. 16) notes that many members of the United States government saw homosexuality as the root of a variety of evils: "Homosexuality, [Senator Joseph R.] McCarthy asserted, was the psychological maladjustment that led people toward communism." Reflecting the broader "homosexual panic" of the moment, both nations explicitly banned immigrants suspected of being homosexual. Locally, police forces were creative in how they used laws to surveil, harass, and arrest individuals engaging in improper sexual and gendered behaviors. Police in the United States would use "masquerade" or "three article" laws to punish anyone thought to be cross-dressing or presenting in an inappropriate way for their perceived sex. In Canada, police relied on similarly archaic legislation to harass homosexuals in the mid twentieth century, regularly citing "vagrancy" or "gross indecency" laws to detain individuals they perceived as deviants. This history shows that, regardless of the legality of certain behaviors, individual police officers have the power to decide the permissibility of acts. In his unpublished memoir, for example, playwright John Herbert writes about being detained by police when dressed in drag in downtown Toronto in the 1950s. The officers told him he was being arrested for appearing in public "disguised by night" – an antiquated law that was included in the 1892 Criminal Code of Canada to deter house burglars who wore masks. These are just some of the legal (and legal-*ish*) methods through which local police forces targeted individuals they perceived as being homosexual in the twentieth century. For local and national governments, homosexuality was considered a social evil that needed to be contained and eradicated.

In the discursive battle over the meaning of homosexuality, social morality, and the acceptable public behaviors related to gender and sexuality that took place in American and Canadian cities in the second half of the twentieth century, collective same-sex dance to popular music played a pivotal role. As archival materials from the 1960s, 1970s, and 1980s show, lesbian and gay liberationists in major North American cities were preoccupied with collective dance, which was simultaneously held up as a method (for fundraising, community building, exploring erotic desires, claiming public space, exhibiting pride in an allegedly abject identity, and more), as well as an ultimate goal. "If I can't dance," posters, pin buttons, t-shirts, and tote bags held at LGBTQ2+ archives in Canada and the United States declare, "I don't want your revolution." D'Emilio (2014, p. 166) writes that "in discos, at women's music festivals, on college campuses, and at street fairs, queer folk looked as if we were dancing our way to freedom." For many homosexuals in these decades, dancing was an aspiration; for agents of the state, it was a target. The fact that repressive governments and self-proclaimed agents of morality were so tormented by same-sex dance throughout these decades should draw our attention to the profound political potential of such collaborative, embodied, and queer acts. To put it bluntly: there were very good reasons that so many people committed to upholding the heteronormative, patriarchal status quo were so concerned about homosexuals dancing together. And for homosexuals, there were even better reasons to fight to make it happen.

1.2 Where Do We Go?

Across North America in the 1960s, 1970s, and 1980s, spaces where homosexuals convened faced sustained surveillance and harassment. Marc Stein (2019, p. 27) argues that bars that permitted homosexual patrons faced multiple simultaneous threats: "straight men targeted them with acts of hate and harassment. Local police conducted raids, demanded payoffs, and engaged in sexual entrapment practices (in which undercover officers enticed men to commit sex crimes and then arrest them) ... State liquor regulators acted against businesses that served 'homosexuals' or permitted 'disorderly,' 'indecent,' or 'lewd' behaviors on their premises." Same-sex intimacy (and its often severe consequences if witnessed by the wrong person) was a primary concern of proprietors and employees of bars and taverns across North America. D'Emilio (2014, p. 166) writes that bars and taverns with homosexual clientele in the 1960s onward "did their own serious policing not just of dancing but of any form of touching. An arm around someone's shoulder or a playful squeeze of someone's butt could be enough to send lurking plainclothes officers into action." This ever present threat of police action meant that bar owners and workers carefully controlled what behaviors were permissible in their venue.

In the grim reality of the 1960s, collective dancing among homosexuals seemed practically impossible. In the unlikely event that homosexuals managed to find a venue that tolerated them – especially one with music and a dance floor whose employees allowed them to move their bodies to the music and where they were allowed to touch or be oriented toward the bodies of others – the threats of a police raid and of being seen and attacked by gay bashers still remained. Despite the risk of violence, of possible arrest and imprisonment, of being taken advantage of by proprietors, and of being outed and shunned, homosexual individuals fought for spaces where they could dance with others.

In February 1970, Chicago Gay Liberation members hosted their first dance at the University of Chicago. According to D'Emilio (2014, p. 167) organizers were pleasantly surprised when over "600 liberated people danced freely to live music." More than one thousand attendees showed up a few months later for another dance on campus. D'Emilio (2014, p. 167) argues that in the early years of lesbian and gay liberation organizing, "the dancing bug was proving contagious." He quotes a newsletter published by Mattachine Midwest that emphasized the political importance of the desire to dance, claiming that "the revolution has just begun, and dances are part of it" (p. 168).[2]

Archival documents, published accounts, and the memories of queer elders indicate that collective social dance was a fundamental component of early lesbian and gay liberation organizing. Indeed, some of the earliest issues of *Come Out!*, the publication of New York City's Gay Liberation Front (GLF), identify collective dance parties as a key element of the group's political activism: "The purpose which we set out for the dances," Kathy Braun (1970, p. 3) writes, is "to provide an alternative to the exploitative gay bars in the city, to raise money for a GLF Community Center, and to politicize the homosexuals hanging around this town." Lesbian and gay dances of the 1970s were often used as fundraisers for the burgeoning community and perceived as a means through which the burgeoning collective could forego exploitative private venues (see Figure 2). But, as Braun makes clear, this is just one function of these dances. In politicizing homosexuals, same-sex dance transformed North American cities during the second half of the 20th century.

2 Dance and Resistance

Music has the capacity to engender feelings of euphoria, belonging, and agency in multiple and complex ways. When we listen and dance to recorded music, we are connected to those who made the recordings, those who are similarly moved by the sound in that space, and to countless others with whom we associate the music. Ray Pratt (1990, p. 7) argues that music is effective in responding to "the desire for a feeling of community," even if that community is imagined. Of course, this also means that music has the capacity to engender feelings of hatred, isolation, and Othering. Music is not inherently good, beautiful, or healing. Nor are the forms of participation and affective states that music evokes universal or ahistorical. But as a medium, music has the capacity to produce and sustain structures of feeling and a steadfast belief that something better is possible.

The sense of intimacy and connectivity elicited by music participation is powerful because it is at once intangible – mental, conceptual, imagined – and profoundly corporeal. The fact that music encourages bodily pleasures and

---

[2] While this framing suggests a progressive narrative – from the oppressive reality of the postwar years to increasingly liberated possibilities of the 1970s and 1980s – it can simultaneously be read as a return to priorities of earlier queer urban subcultures. As George Chauncey (1994) argues, social networks of homosexuals, many of which were built around dance, flourished in New York City in the early twentieth century. What makes the gay embrace of collective dance of the 1970s and 1980s unique, however, is that many activists perceived same-sex social dance as vital to lesbian and gay liberation and the consciousness-raising process necessary to change individuals' minds.

Figure 2 "Lesbiantics" published by E. Bedoz (Ellen Shumsky) in the Dec/January 1970 issue of *Come Out! A Liberation Forum for the Gay Community* shows how community organized dances challenged the dominance of exploitative private bars and taverns.

connects individuals in intimate ways is one of the reasons that music and dance have long been considered menacing threats to social order. Ann Louise Wagner (1997, p. xiii) argues that three primary characteristics of dancing make it promising for revolution and thus a target of regressive political attacks. First, "dancing involves the human body"; second, "powerful sexual stimulation can come into play" when musical rhythms influence movement; and third, dance tends to occur outside of labor under capitalism, meaning that dancers are not producing material goods or services.

Emergent forms of social dance in North America have regularly been perceived as threatening to the status quo, even when the style of dance seems, from our current vantage point, emblematic of ostensibly proper social behaviors. This is particularly apparent when dance is linked with anxieties around gender, sexuality, and race. Steven Baur (2008, p. 47), for example, discusses the concerns that circulated in late nineteenth-century America around young women who danced the waltz – a practice, social critics argued, that "could damage their health and destroy their social prospects." He quotes the New York City chief of police who, in 1880, "claimed that 'three-fourths of the abandoned girls in New York were ruined by dancing'" (p. 49).[3] For some critics, dance is threatening precisely because of the way it enlivens bodily and sexual pleasures in public. For dancers, recognizing that shared bodily experiences of music enable new, seemingly improper ways of understanding one's body can bring cultural norms and expectations into question.

When social dance is taken up by marginalized communities this threat is often perceived as intensified, intersecting with concerns about reproduction, order, and the menacing sexual proclivities of others that threaten to upend systems of white heteropatriarchy. Dance is an overt manifestation of embodied desire and shared eroticism that can reify conventional social relations or imagine alternatives to the status quo. Jane C. Desmond (1997, p. 7) argues that "with its linkage to sex, sexiness, and sexuality, dance provides a dense and fecund field for investigating how sexualities are inscribed, learned, rendered, and continually resignified through bodily actions." Dance that challenges so-called proper sexual and gender behaviors can thus be world-making, capable of eliciting emergent forms of pleasure and aberrant relations.

Concerns about allegedly proper gender and sexual behaviors inform the long history of suspicion and denunciation of social dance. As Susan McClary (2007, p. 204) has shown, the way that music "intersects with the body and destabilizes accepted norms of subjectivity, gender, and sexuality—is precisely where the

---

[3] Police have made similar claims in the twentieth century as well: according to Will Straw (2014, n.p.), police in Montreal, Quebec, "reported in 1970 that 80% of Montreal's missing young people could be found in discotheques."

politics of music reside." This is particularly apparent throughout history when music serves as a spark for collective, embodied experiences for oppressed groups. McClary (2007, p. 204) links this directly to music and dance practices of marginalized communities, arguing that there is a "musical power of the disenfranchised" that has to do with a collective "ability to articulate different ways of construing the body ... that bring along in their wake the potential for different experiential worlds." That music and dance practices of marginalized communities regularly invite anxious and aggressive responses from arbiters of morality reveals the transformative and political potential of such acts.

In the case of lesbian and gay liberation, dancing and the associated imagining of alternative futures was the bedrock of political organizing and as such posed a grave threat to the social ideologies and the moral order of the era. Experiences on the dance floor typically involve multiple processes of becoming: dancers explore their own desires and expressions of self in creative and playful ways while simultaneously creating the broader communities to which they feel an affinity. However, accessing spaces that enabled this – and the feelings of belonging that could be attained therein – was not always simple or safe; the violent reactions to dancing groups of lesbians and gays throughout the twentieth century show the power of dance to challenge the status quo. As a result, bars that allowed entry to gay and lesbian patrons often found themselves in the crosshairs of police across North America – especially if the venue permitted dancing.

A 1967 article in *Tangents*, written by Jim Highland, provides a particularly troubling example of police intervention in underground gay dance spaces. Around midnight on New Year's Eve in 1966, undercover police raided the Black Cat, a popular gay bar on Sunset Boulevard in Los Angeles. When the raid began, police immediately targeted the source of the music, ripping the jukebox's plug out of the wall. Then, Highland (1967, p. 5) writes, they used the machine as a weapon, throwing a dancer "headfirst against the jukebox. It was a heavy machine but the impact jarred it away from the wall." Highland explains that, as is often the case in such raids, police behaved particularly brutally against people they perceived as transgressing normative gender roles.

Police forces in other major North American cities were similarly aggressive in how they surveilled and disciplined same-sex dancing. On January 1, 1965, "dozens of police swarmed in and around California Hall in San Francisco on New Year's Day, invading a benefit costume ball organized by the Council on Religion and the Homosexual" (Tobin, 1965, p. 4). Rusty's – the most popular lesbian bar in Philadelphia – was raided by police on March 8, 1968. According to writers identified as A. B. and C. F., who wrote about the event in the *Daughters of Bilitis Philadelphia Newsletter*, "no minors were found on the premises [and] there were no apparent violations of existing laws"; rather, the police raided the premises because the "couples dancing to the jukebox ... were all female" ("Editorial," 1968, p. 1). In March 1966, when Los Angeles police raided the Yukon, a small bar on Beverly Boulevard, they first "yanked the jukebox cord and ordered the lights up ... [one officer] announced, 'we're going to make a few arrests ... Anyone who runs will be shot'" ("Anatomy of a Raid," 1968, p. 8). Dancers at these events were targeted by police because of their allegedly immoral physical encounters animated by musical sound, movement, and nonnormative sexual desires. In many of these examples, police interrupt the music to quickly thwart the possibilities of collective dance, drawing our attention to the underlying political force of music in its capacity to enliven bodies and animate a collective.

Part of what makes social dance so dangerous to oppressive systems of categorization and social order is that it has the capacity to imbue participants with a sense of individual and collective agency without requiring uniformity or stability of the group in question. Uncontainable, infectious, and euphoric, the feelings attainable on a dance floor are not exclusively based on identification, stability, and sameness, but on a fleeting affiliation with others who are similarly enlivened by musical sound and the embodied forms of togetherness that such experiences induce. For Garcia-Mispireta (2023, pp. 5, 33), a sense of "vague belonging" among heterogeneous dance crowds enables what he calls "liquidarity, a form of fluid solidarity" that creates conditions for collective emergence and cohesion without requiring homogeneity. For Shank (2014, p. 9), the possibility of belonging across difference is fundamental to music's beauty and political force: "when you and I hit the dance floor together, listening to the elegant dynamism of a perfect beat, we will feel a community that will never be exactly the same for either of us. The force of that difference is what propels us." Dance floor relationality – corporeal, fleeting, dynamic, and comprised of difference – can challenge categorization and be beautifully queer.[4]

For Sara Ahmed (2006, p. 106), experiences that engender queer possibility are necessarily fleeting "given that the straight world is already in place." "Our response," she argues, "need not be to search for permanence ... but to listen to the sound of 'the what' that fleets" (p. 106). Obsession with identity has hoodwinked us into thinking that queerness is something we *are* rather than something we *do*, but the promise of queerness has always been that it is a relentless process of invention and reinvention. Queer thinkers have long

---

[4] The framework I'm articulating here didn't exist at the time in question. Indeed, as historian Steven Maynard elucidates in his generative critique of this framing, activists in the early years of the lesbian and gay liberation period were pushing homosexuality as a stable individual and communal identity. I'm not interested in attempting to reconcile this dissonance; instead, I want to hold on to the multiplicity of lenses and the way activists of the past were building a kind of blueprint for us in the present. S. Maynard, personal communication, February 2023.

identified the promise of understanding queerness as a momentary disruption (Sullivan 2022, p. 4) and an "affiliative ... set of relations, lived and imagined" (Nealon, 2001, p. 180). To imagine queerness as a set of relations, a mode of being-with, or a momentary connection with others, is to be open to unknowable queer futures and the ways that even the smallest acts are performatively productive for the dynamic collective project of queerness. This is a particularly generative way to approach the past and to honor the diverse collectives that brought the present into being.

Linear approaches to history that compel stable identification tend to ossify people into fixed groups in order to make sense of their relationships to events. However, privileging an affiliative relationality in the way we study the past grants the people in those histories the same complexities and freedoms we allow ourselves in the queer present: people change and their affiliations and desires shift. We should retrain ourselves to seek out alternative forms of historical evidence: queer desires, fleeting affiliations, and embodied collective experiences that sparked feelings of bliss and possibility. In his essay "Ephemera as Evidence," Muñoz (1996, p. 6) reminds us that "queerness is often transmitted covertly ... as innuendo, gossip, fleeting moments, and performances that are meant to be interacted with by those within its epistemological sphere—while evaporating at the touch of those who would eliminate queer possibility." Attuning our ears to hear these traces and fading echoes allows alternative narratives to emerge.

As we examine histories of queer life, these alternative forms of evidence are poised to undermine and move beyond dominant historical narratives. An attention to music and dance must be a key component in how we attend to the history of lesbian and gay liberation. Indeed, for many individuals, dance ignited a desire for liberation and allowed them to experience – for a moment – what life could feel like. Framing music and dance as the germ for new affiliations and as a dangerously powerful and collaborative activity allows us access to alternative and unrecognized narratives of queer formation and transformation. Even the most well-established stories of lesbian and gay liberation in North America are enriched by an attention to musical sounds and practices.

2.1 Spinning Historical Records

The story of the Stonewall Riots is well known within LGBTQ2+ communities and in the broader, straighter world.[5] The Stonewall Inn in Greenwich Village,

---

[5] In 2016, President Barack Obama designated the venue and its surrounding area a national monument to commemorate the 1969 riots – the first explicitly gay-oriented national monument in the nation's history. Stonewall's dominance in histories of lesbian and gay liberation is not unique to the United States. Many nations that celebrate Pride Week or Month do so in June,

New York City, was a social hangout for a diverse collective of individuals marginalized by sexual desire and gender expression, including people we would now identify as street-involved and homeless youth, trans and gender-nonconforming individuals, and gay men and lesbians belonging to various categories of age, race, and class. Like most bars that permitted such clientele, the Stonewall Inn was frequently raided by local police (despite the generous payoffs they received from the venue's owners). In the early hours of June 28, 1969, undercover and uniformed officers served a warrant as per their usual practice of harassment. According to Stein (2019, p. 3), "there were approximately two hundred people in the bar" when this raid began and police "detained several bar employees, patrons without identification, butches, transvestites, and people who talked back or fought back; they told everyone else to leave." Many of the patrons who were pushed out of the venue milled around on Christopher Street and, as the police continued their work inside, the crowd outside the bar grew both in size and agitation. When police attempted to leave the Stonewall Inn, the crowd refused safe passage and the officers were forced to retreat into the bar. Eventually, a tactical squad arrived and attempted to clear the large, angry crowd that had convened. As Stein (2019, p. 5) describes: "over the next several hours, thousands of people rioted in the streets with campy courage and fierce fury." This first night of the riots lasted a few hours, but it sparked something larger that sustained activists. Riots took place over the next several days and, as the story goes, the gay liberation movement was born.

While we collectively risk overemphasizing its role in the formation of the gay liberation movement – after all, it was not the first time that queer people had rioted in response to police violence – the Stonewall uprising had a profound effect on life in New York City and beyond. Within months of the riots, gay liberation newspapers (including *Gay Power*, *Out*, and *Gay*) were started and political blocs (most famously the GLF and the Queens Liberation Front) formed. As Michael Denneny (2023, p. 5) argues, publications and organizations in this moment were a direct response to the Stonewall Riots, representing various "attempts to establish a public forum for the gay community ... and evaluate what was happening to us and around us."

In his impressive work titled *The Stonewall Riots*, Stein (2019, p. 14) identifies several "interpretive frameworks" that "help us to understand why the Stonewall Riots occurred when and where they did." He points to the homophile movement of the mid twentieth century and its radicalization in the late 1960s; a long history of resistance at bars and similar venues; other social movements

---

marking the anniversary of the Stonewall Riots; indeed, while Canadian activists first convened in August to mark the anniversary of the August 28, 1971, gay rights rally in Ottawa, in the late twentieth century most Pride celebrations in the nation moved to June.

of the era (including women's liberation, Black power politics, and antiwar movements); and "the combination of heightened expectations and dashed hopes that many felt as the country transitioned from a period of liberal reform to one of conservative backlash" that included "a new wave of police raids, violent killings, and local vigilantism" (pp. 14–15). These are all important lenses through which we can better understand the Stonewall Riots and their broader context. However, the music and music cultures of the Stonewall Inn are unmentioned – an unfortunate oversight because music participation offers another interpretive framework to better understand the Stonewall Riots and the conditions under which they occurred.

The Stonewall Inn was, by most accounts, a foul space run by a management team that had little respect for customers. As Stein (2019, p. 3) writes: "patrons complained about high prices, watered-down drinks, dirty glasses, and unclean facilities." Despite this, the Stonewall Inn was hugely popular with a diverse group of queer patrons who were marginalized by broader cultural ideologies around gender, sexuality, race, and class. One reason why this bar was well-attended, despite its obvious shortcomings, is that it was widely known as a bar that permitted gender play, subtle acts of sexual deviancy, and queer dance.

Several memoirs by lesbian and gay liberation activists identify the Stonewall Inn as the city's prime dance location. Puerto Rican actor and singer Holly Woodlawn (1991, p. 110) writes about the venue in her memoir, noting that "inside it was very dark, with a long bar to one side and go-go boys in bikinis dancing on either end. It had a dance floor and a jukebox. The place attracted an eclectic bunch: butch guys, preppy boys, older men, a few lesbians, and a few so-called straight men sprinkled in between." Trans activists also claimed space on the venue's dance floor. Edmund White (2009, p. 51) writes of the "long-legged, fierce-eyed antics of the STAR members (Street Transvestite Action Revolutionaries)" who often danced at the venue. Historians have also noted the appeal of the dance floor at the Stonewall Inn. Martin Duberman (1993, p. 225) argues that what made the Stonewall "the most popular gay bar in Greenwich Village" in the late 1960s was that it "was also the only gay male bar in New York where dancing was permitted."

The Stonewall Inn had two dance spaces, demarcated by the type of music played and the forms of bodily participation that the music encouraged. David Carter (2004, p. 73) writes that a jukebox in the front area of the bar "offered more mainstream performers such as the Beach Boys." In his book *Stonewall: The Riots that Sparked the Gay Revolution*, Carter (2004, p. 73) quotes Thomas Lanigan-Schmidt, who explains that "some people called the front room 'the white room' because of its racial makeup and its music." Patrons that Carter interviewed referred to the back room as the "Black" or "Puerto Rican room" because the jukebox there was stocked with dance-oriented music structured around repetitive grooves. Carter (2004, p. 73) argues that this back room was the favored space of "homeless youth, as well as young Blacks and Puerto Ricans" who would dance the night away at the Stonewall.

Musicologists, scholars of sound, and cultural geographers have shown how sound *creates* social space. Brandon LaBelle (2010, p. xxi), for example, emphasizes the power of sound to demarcate space, condition individuals in certain ways, and connect people in the sonic register; he argues that sound forms "links, groupings, and conjunctions that accentuate individual identity as a relational project. The flows of surrounding sonority can be heard to weave an individual into a large social fabric, filling relations with local sound, sonic culture, auditory memories, and the noises that move between, contributing to the making of shared spaces." Simultaneously, music can initiate collectives, elicit new forms of relationships, and produce spatial understanding.

It's the back room at the Stonewall Inn that I'm most interested in, the one filled with enthusiastic dancers who find their way to the rear of the bar and, in the process, alter their relationships to their bodies and the world they inhabit. The music of this room, with its repetitive groove-induced sense of presentness, allowed dancers to suspend everyday temporality and access a sense of belonging and freedom. In this space, we can imagine the beautiful queer encounters that Muñoz (2013, p. 103) encourages us to reach for: those sparked by "a visceral desire to want something else within a field of ossified social relations." Dance floors can foment something else – something more.

The Stonewall Inn was *the* place to dance in Greenwich Village in 1969, but it was not a utopian or consistently safe dance space. While the venue offered dancers and drinkers feelings of blissful possibility, it also regularly conveyed how quickly that sense of possibility could be shattered. Like most bars that allowed lesbian and gay patrons, the Stonewall Inn had an elaborate alarm system to warn staff and patrons of an impending police raid. Duberman (1993, p. 231) writes that the Stonewall's main dancing area was "lit only with black lights." While this provided a trippy ambience for the dance floor, the light was more practical: when uniformed police arrived – or when someone suspected of being a plainclothes undercover police officer entered the club – "white bulbs instantly came on in the dance area, signaling everyone to stop dancing or touching" (p. 232). A visual warning sign was a common practice in venues that permitted homosexual clientele as a change in lighting was the quickest way to signal dancers to separate and straighten up.[6]

---

[6] In *Gay Bar*, Jeremy Atherton Lin (2021, p. 77) describes a sonic signal that The Patch, a gay bar in Los Angeles, used in the late 1960s: the venue's proprietor Lee Gaze would "put 'God Save the

A few days after the riots, in a *New York Post* article, Jay Levin (1969, p. 36) writes that the Stonewall Inn was "the mecca of gay night life. Behind its blacked out windows, the gay young men drank, danced, and made attachments with confidence that, at last, they had found sanctuary." According to Stonewall regulars, the place really did feel like a place of refuge. Lanigan-Schmidt tells Jason Baumann (2019, p. 106) that he and his friends felt "safe and sound" at the Stonewall; he recalls that "the jukebox played a lot of Motown music. We danced... Here the consciousness of knowing you 'belonged' nestled into that warm feeling of finally being home. And home engenders love and loyalty quite naturally, so we loved the Stonewall" (see Figure 3).

Because it permitted same-sex dancing, the Stonewall Inn attracted a cross-section of queer patrons that might not have otherwise been brought together. For Michael Warner (1999, pp. 35–36), this is one of the hallmarks of a queer scene that allows a special kind of sociality: "queer scenes are the true *salons des refusés*, where the most heterogeneous people are brought into great intimacy by their common experience of being despised and rejected in a world of norms that they now recognize as false morality." It was this heterogeneity that imbued the Stonewall with the sense of collective power and that animated the Stonewall Riots. Indeed, one of the most profound aspects of dance floor experience is that it can engender a sense of collectivity without erasing difference – on the dance floor, belonging across difference can manifest and challenge simplistic homogeneous notions of queerness. On the dance floor, queer participants can perceive the ways they are different from heteronormative society (and its ideals) as well as from others moving to the music. On the dance floor, one's sense of community can constantly be formed, contested, and reformed. Lanigan-Schmidt describes the raids that sparked the riots, writing that "it was not only a raid but a bust... the lights went on. It wasn't a pretty sight ... the music box [was] broken. The dancing stopped ... Nobody thought of it as history, herstory, my-story, your-story, or our-story. We were being denied a place to dance together. That's all" (quoted in in Baumann, 2019, p. 107).

Lanigan-Schmidt makes clear that the police's violation of this sacred space and their attempt to deny him and his fellow patrons "a place to dance together" was a breaking point. Dancing allowed patrons a way to feel good and a part of something in a world that disallowed this recognition at every turn. As Garcia-Mispireta (2014, n.p.) argues, queer dance spaces of the 1970s and 1980s "are places where the injustices and indignities of everyday life can be not only temporarily relieved but to some extent redressed ... their dance floors ...

Queen' on the jukebox to indicate that members of the vice squad were present, signaling the crowd to cease shows of affection."

Figure 3 A group of patrons in front of the Stonewall Inn. Photograph by Fred W. McDarrah/MUUS Collection.

provide concrete sites for the collective envisioning of a different kind of 'good life.'" Many people thought such feelings, and the venues that sparked them, were worth fighting for.

Archival materials and personal accounts give us a partial sense of the Stonewall Inn's musical soundscape. The music that played the back room was up-tempo soul (both Southern soul and Northern soul Motown), as well as funk. I've previously observed the importance of repetitive musical grooves in this history (Jennex, 2020, p. 420), a device that other musicologists reference as well: Robert Walser (1995, p. 209) notes the "joy in repetition" of African American popular music dance traditions that sustain rhythmic tensions, and Anne Danielsen (2006, p. 144) argues that repetitive grooves can "engender an intense, almost euphoric feeling" that is outside of the temporality of the everyday. Through participation in certain music, dancers can be out of time *together*. A document produced by the Stonewall Veterans' Association lists the most popular songs on Stonewall jukeboxes during the week of the famous riots and helps to elucidate the function of music in the venue and this history. Number one on this chart is the 1969 hit "No Matter What Sign You Are" by Diana Ross and the Supremes. Duberman (1993, p. 233) seems to verify this ranking, noting that "the Motown label was still top of the heap" at the Stonewall in the "summer of 1969." Musicologist Jap Kooijman (2002, n.p.) writes that "No Matter What Sign You Are," "while less popular with mainstream audience ... proved to be very successful in the underground gay scene. In fact," he writes, "'No Matter What Sign You Are' was the number-one hit single at the Stonewall Inn ... the night that the famous gay bar was raided by the New York police."

It is not just that marginalized people could dance at the Stonewall Inn; when we examine collective dance experiences of the past, the type of music matters. As I discuss above, collective dance has long been understood as a threat to the moral and social order precisely because of the feelings of embodied sexual freedom and collective belonging that it can evoke. However, to understand the specificity of the way dance encourages feelings of bliss and resistance, we must parse specific musical details. We need to listen closely and feel the groove.

2.2 Good Vibration

"No Matter What Sign You Are" renders audible popular aesthetics of the historical moment from which it emerges, simultaneously referencing traditions of psychedelic music popular in the 1960s, as well as the cyclical rhythmic grooves and symphonic sound of the burgeoning soul subgenres that laid the groundwork for what would become known as disco. While credited as backing vocalists, the Supremes are not heard on this recording. Like many of the songs ostensibly featuring the Supremes, "No Matter What Sign You Are" featured studio vocalists supporting Ross's lead vocals. In this case, the backup singers heard on the recording are the Blackberries – Venetta Fields, Sherlie Matthews, and Clydie King – an in-demand trio of Black women vocalists who provided support for many of the artists and groups who recorded at Motown's West Coast studios. Motown's house band The Funk Brothers, a shifting group of session musicians, provided instrumental backing for the track. The labor of many talented performers makes this song what it is; Ross may be a queen, but this song is a communal endeavor.

"No Matter What Sign You Are" opens with a brief introductory phrase performed on a Coral sitar, an electric guitar designed to mimic the sound of a traditional sitar – a plucked string instrument with a long history in South Asian music performance. Following the sitar's two-bar opening phrase, played freely without giving a sense of the song's time signature or rhythmic groove, a snare drum fill demands listeners' attention and soon settles into a full drum beat that delineates both the song's tempo and groove. The backing vocals enter as soon as the drummer establishes the song's regular tempo – the Blackberries sing the twelve-star signs as Ross provides vocal flourishes between their delivery.

Ross sings "the moon shines bright above" slightly in advance of the verse so that her delivery of "bright" is heard on the downbeat of the first bar. Lyrically, the song describes feelings of nighttime connection that resist systems of classification meant to keep people apart: "no matter what sign you are / you're gonna be mine, you are." As Ross exclaims, we "can't let astrology chart our destiny . . . the beat of the heart, my love / is stronger than the charts, my love." The song's lyrics, which encourage listeners to permit themselves forbidden forms of intimacy, make this song easily applicable to the queer connections on the Stonewall Inn's dance floor. "No Matter What Sign You Are" also exhibits the sound of feminine collectivity, with backup singers supporting the lead singer's disclosure of prohibited love and desire in a style of collective vocal performance that Jacqueline Warwick (2007, p. 46) theorizes as "girl talk." While Ross's voice is the focal point of the verses, backup singers repeat her concluding lyrics at the end of each phrase and perform audible signals of active listening to the lead – in this way, they simultaneously codify girl group practices of vocal texture and remain present throughout as a support system for the lead.

It's not just the lyrical content of the song that made it well-suited for the dance floor of the Stonewall Inn. Indeed, "No Matter What Song You Are" encourages collective bodily expression and kinetic movement. The drummer plays sixteenth notes on the hi-hat – with subtle accents on beats one and three – and pounds a backbeat on the snare on beats two and four. In other words, in this conventional sixteenth note rock beat, listeners hear a familiar (straight) rock groove; the drummer is accenting beats one, two, three, and four, in each bar on either the hi-hat or the snare drum. The effect of this is that the drums provide a consistent articulation of the groove and make it easy and comfortable to dance to the music.[7]

---

[7] Some 1960s soul, disco, and subsequent dance musics feature a "four-on-the-floor" bass drum groove (in which the four beats of a bar are pounded on the bass drum) as genre markers for this very reason: a consistent and simple beat gives dancers a shared framework for bodily expression. The four-on-the-floor bass drumbeat serves to bind together a previously disorganized collective

Ultimately, "No Matter What Sign You Are" is both playful and impactful, articulating the potential of unapproved connections and evoking a dance music collective through sonic properties. This is a particular moment in the history of dance music: one before live DJs became commonplace. The way the music is projected in the Stonewall Inn in 1969 is different from that of other dance floor experiences I unpack in this Element, as music at this venue was played through a jukebox rather than by a live DJ. This means that music stopped at the end of each song as the device readied the next single. Each of these songs, then, was played as an individual piece of music, followed by a few seconds of silence and the faint sounds of the machine preparing the next selection. From the 1970s on, DJs manipulated musical recordings so that this silence was no longer necessary: moving between two turntables meant that a DJ could keep music playing consistently, curating a suite of music that lasted much longer than a single EP or LP. While some artists were playing with crossfading methods in recorded albums of the 1960s to eliminate this silence between tracks and give the sense of a continuous live performance – The Beatles' 1967 album *Sgt. Pepper's Lonely Hearts Club Band* is the first and perhaps most famous example – crossfading during live DJ sets would not become common practice for a few more years. At the Stonewall Inn, environmental sound – patrons chatting, bottles clinking, music from the venue's other jukebox bleeding into the back room – would fill the silence between songs. Maybe some dancers would continue moving their bodies to keep energized and in the groove before the next song began. Imagine the anticipation in these moments; dancers waiting, expectant and excited for the music to begin again – sharing brief moments of longing for what is to come.

The rhythmic circularity of the vast majority of music heard in the back room of the Stonewall allowed dancers to feel lifted out of the present and into extraordinary musical time. Being out of time can feel like a powerful experience. Being out of time with others can change everything. The transformation of such an experience can make a return to the normative oppressive nature of the everyday difficult to handle. While the Stonewall Inn was a site of regular police raids, Duberman (1993, p. 239) writes that the one that sparked the infamous riots occurred at "one-twenty A.M.—the height of the merriment, and much later than usual raids." In other words: the raids that sparked the infamous Stonewall Riots occurred long after dancers had experienced musical time on the dance floor, and after they accessed the hopeful, transformative effects of collective dance to repetitive, groove-based music that binds dancers

---

of bodies. In the same way a conductor articulates the beats of a bar to provide a temporal structure for orchestral musicians, the simple bass drumbeat offers dancers a shared timing.

together across forms of difference. The structures of feeling enabled by intimacy and camaraderie on the dance floor allowed participants to register a different, more free arrangement that they were not ready to relinquish when they lights turned on and police barged in.

As a reevaluation of the narrative of the Stonewall Riots shows, powerful feelings of bliss, belonging, and individual and collective agency can be made tangible through dance. As a result, forms of social dance that challenge conventions of heteronormativity, patriarchy, and white supremacy are so often targeted by those committed to established traditions of morality and the prevailing status quo. Collective dance – perhaps especially when practiced by marginalized communities – can be a spark that ignites feelings of solidarity and the drive to resist. This potential becomes particularly evident in lesbian and gay history in the 1970s as liberatory politics and dance music and culture mature together in cities across North America.

3 Dancing to Liberation

Collective dance music culture and the lesbian and gay liberation movement both matured during the 1970s, but these histories are often cleaved. There was, the story goes, political organizing on the one hand, and on the other, underground dance cultures that offered a sense of escape and relief from stultifying cultural realities. While some scholars identify the political utility of dance floor pleasures for broader ideals of gay liberation,[8] these movements are widely remembered as concurrent but distinct. I suspect this separation occurs because the forms of collectivity and sociality afforded by dance music cultures do not fit neatly into the privileged, progressive narrative of lesbian and gay rights.

Carnal pleasures are often expunged from histories of political progress. This is unfortunate, as experiences of erotic bliss are often the things that spark desire for social change. Denneny (2023, p. 2) argues that "historians will probably concentrate on the history of organizations and political heroes—how the Gay Liberation Front led to the Gay Activists Alliance led to the National Gay Task Force, how Frank Kameny challenged the state, a story of laws passed, elections contested, court battles won and lost—and, of course, this is history." But what really changed in the wake of the Stonewall Riots, Denneny (2023, p. 2) argues, was a shift in how gay people understood their bodies and their bodily capacities: "after decades of repression a whole generation suddenly felt free to explore what had been forbidden ... the exhilaration and entanglements of

---

[8] See, for example, Allen (2009) and (2021), D'Emilio (2014), Dyer (1979), Echols (2010), Garcia-Mispireta (2014), Hilderbrand (2023), Lawrence (2004, 2011), Niebur (2022), Nyong'o (2008), and Roman (2011), among others.

sex and romance were what preoccupied and bedeviled me and most of my gay friends in the early Seventies."

Dance music cultures of the 1970s and 1980s provide echoes of a queer past that occurred before assimilationist politics took hold of the LGBTQ2+ movement, and by examining the music and dance experiences we can unearth some of these histories that have since been rewritten with different emphases. For example, before the mainstreaming and whitewashing of disco culture, it was characterized by a coalitional politics that is increasingly difficult to recognize in the present (in part because it manifested on the dance floor, outside of what is today considered "legitimate" political space). Today, homonormative ideals have pervaded mainstream LGBTQ2+ organizing and broader social discourse to the detriment of queer notions of difference, plurality, and fleeting manifestations of collective political power, and so this past becomes radically productive, even crucial. Something we risk forgetting is that the dance floors of the lesbian and gay liberation era encouraged a sense of embodied, erotic, and transformative plurality for minoritarian individuals and afforded them with alternative ways of being in the world with others. Before acceptable gay identities were entrenched in the cultural imaginations of most North American citizens, people perceived as gay and lesbian faced precarious access to safety and security. It is not a time that we would want to return to – nor is it one we could return to even if we wanted. But looking closely at a time before gay and lesbian liberation morphed into what currently exists in mainstream North American culture as LGBTQ2+ politics can animate what we understand as possible for queer life.

In his classic article "In Defence of Disco," Richard Dyer (1979) identified the queer force of disco at a time that it was being dismissed or outrightly attacked by figures across a broad political spectrum. Public critiques from the right often focused on disco culture's ubiquity and excessiveness; more covert or implied critiques vilified it through its association with certain marginalized communities including people of color (especially Black and Latinx citizens), queers, and others in urban areas of major cities. From more leftist perspectives, disco's ubiquity and mainstreaming was a detriment that was spoiling its once unique potential. At the end of the 1970s, a farcical counterfeit version of what was once a secret and subversive way of understanding and articulating oneself in relation to music and culture dominated the mainstream; even worse, the poor imitation and the audiences associated with it were the epitome of ordinary, normal, conventional life.[9] In this context, Dyer identified disco as politically

---

[9] By the end of the 1970s, Peter Shapiro (2005, p. 222) argues, disco participation was basically "hearing 'YMCA' six times in one night at the Rainbow Room of the Holiday Inn in Cedar Rapids, Iowa, while doing line dances with a bunch of travelling salesmen."

useful and worthy of scrutiny and sustained analysis on the left. He made his arguments in *New Left*, an alternative journal produced by and for socialist gay men in London (despite the fact that socialists offered some of the most vociferous critiques of disco music and culture coming out of lesbian and gay liberation thought).[10] For Dyer (1979, p. 23), disco music culture reflects and constructs a shared sense of collectivity and agency among marginalized populations – a political function of the musical genre that is particularly clear in the mid-1970s when "non-commercial discos organized by gay and women's groups" flourished in urban spaces. Yes, he concedes, disco could be used for capitalist, materialist, and regressive means, but so too could it be used to make perceptible a sense of possibility for people desirous of a more economically and socially just world. For him, disco's three main characteristics of eroticism, romanticism, and materialism are – like musical culture as a whole – not inherently good or bad. But the way that these characteristics come together in dance spaces organized by marginalized communities can enable collective recognition of what could (and should) be. "If it feels good," Dyer writes, "use it" (p. 23).

Following the discursive shift around gay liberation, identity, and community that occurred in the late 1960s and early 1970s, burgeoning lesbian and gay movements in cities around North America did indeed use disco in a way that capitalized on the music's productive elements that Dyer identifies. In places we might expect, like New York and Toronto, active and coordinated lesbian and gay organizations created collective dance opportunities that reshaped their political communities and settings. But we can also see this in smaller cities across North America in ways that underscore the productive relationship forged between collective dance cultures and lesbian and gay liberation politics outside of major urban centers.

Disco has multiple histories and disparate trajectories. Jafari S. Allen (2021, p. 118) argues that disco "contains multitudes" and "cannot be confined to one moment or trajectory." Indeed, the DJs I interviewed about dance experiences of the 1970s shied away from the term "disco," usually opting for the more nebulous "dance music" to describe their work. Bob Stout told me that he played music for people to dance to and was largely unconcerned with distinctions in relation to musical genres and sub genres. Despite music industry insiders' attempts to codify and monetize the genre, there was always profound variation in the sound of music that is often classified disco. This is not a bad

---

[10] Luis-Manuel Garcia-Mispireta, in his article "Richard Dyer, 'In Defence of Disco' (1979)," and Jaap Kooijman in "Turn the Beat Around: Richard Dyer's 'In Defence of Disco' Revisited" both articulate the context of Dyer's (1979) work and, in so doing, compellingly present the article as a foundational and generative text.

thing: in dance music – as is the case for queerness – amorphousness is generative. Vince Aletti (2018, p. 7) argues that, "especially early on, the music had no dominant style and that's what made it so interesting: it was coming from all over, but mainly underground, and a lot of the most successful club records never made it to radio."

In this section, I focus on dance music sounds, structures, and the forms of participation the music invites. Disco prioritizes palpable feelings of presentness and alternative experiences of time. The experiences enabled by participation in the music and culture can be transformative – and the fact that such experiences happen alongside others on the dance floor allows participants to rethink their relations in a broad sense. Recognizing the experience as shared is vital to understanding the political force of collective dance, because it positions queerness as a dynamic process of becoming that gains its meaning by nature of its being shared. Collectives that formed at the intersection of dance music culture and lesbian and gay liberation politics of the 1970s emphasized an interdependence that bound dancers and DJs in a process of creation and revelation – the latter of which refers to both a luxuriating and a discovering.

In the 1970s, lesbian and gay liberationists across North America were increasingly critical of private venues that preyed on homosexuals. New York City's GLF activist Jerry Hoose (qtd. in Teal, 1971, pp. 57–58) contends that the first dance the group organized was directly in response to exploitative practices by owners of private bars; he remembers that "we sat down and started thinking about the oppression we faced in the bars that we went to, the things we had to deal with nightly … and we decided that this dance was going to get us completely away from that." As Don Teal (1971, p. 58) explains, the GLF's first dance signaled a shift of what was possible in New York City. At this event at Alternate University, a leftist counterculture school in Greenwich Village, "gays were hosting gays—not capitalizing on them—and the spirit of the militants infected all non-gay-lib visitors, making the dances a real celebration of life." He quotes an unnamed gay activist who exclaimed, "at a dance, the vibrations are certainly a lot better than at a bar."

The GLF's first women-only dance – held in April 1970 – exemplifies the stranglehold Mafia-controlled bars had on gays and lesbians in New York City at the time. Karla Jay (1999, p. 129) writes that "several extremely large men in trench coats with guns in their belts" burst into the venue around 3 a.m. as volunteers were cleaning up after the dance. Pandemonium broke out as drug users rushed to hide or flush narcotics and women who were undocumented escaped through the back door of the venue. The men flashed their badges and started beating women, directing their ire at the more butch women present. Jay managed to leave the venue, find a telephone, and call Florynce Kennedy, a "radical African American lesbian lawyer [who] had given [Jay] her number and said to call her in case of trouble at the dance" (p. 130). Kennedy immediately called the police and the press, and when the media arrived at the dance, the violent, armed men left. When NYPD officers arrived moments later, they confirmed that the men who arrived with guns and badges were not police officers. It quickly dawned on the women that the violent thugs were working on behalf of two local lesbian bars that were controlled by organized crime groups. In the June/July 1970 issue of *Come Out!*, Kathy Wakeham (1970, p. 9) reported on the event and highlighted the way the harassment shows the importance of the community-organized dances, writing that "the purpose of the dance was to give our sisters an alternative to the oppressive Mafia-controlled gay bars." Rather than scaring the women into walking away from organizing dances, the harassment strengthened their resolve and underscored the need for community-run events (see Figure 4).

For Jay (1999, p. 90), the problem with bars was not simply that they were exploitative, unwelcoming, and unsafe, but that they were conventionally "divided along gender lines" and disallowed any sense of solidarity between gay men and lesbians. Keeping members of a marginalized community segregated based on identifications such as race, gender, class, and sex means that the whole is rendered invisible. Recognizing the sheer size of a collective can be a powerful thing, at once indicating that one is not alone and that there is power in numbers.[11] This is particularly important when the collective is comprised both through and across difference.

Figure 4 Volunteers at the GLF's women-only dance at Alternate University in Greenwich Village in 1970. Manuscript and Archives Division, The New York Public Library. Photograph by Diana Davies.

---

[11] In *The Motion of Light in Water*, Samuel Delany (2004, p. 293) argues that "the first direct sense of political power comes from the apprehension of massed bodies." Delany writes of his experiences

3.1 Meet Me at The Turret

In the early to mid 1970s, the gay and lesbian social scene in the city of Halifax, Nova Scotia, was relatively minor. The few spaces that did exist for lesbian and gay sociality in Halifax in the early and mid 1970s were under surveillance by police and largely segregated in terms of gender, race, and class. Robin Metcalfe, a former executive member of the Gay Alliance for Equality (GAE) – the city's lesbian and gay liberation community group that formed in 1972 – and a historian and archivist of queer culture in Nova Scotia, tells me that he and other white men would spend their time at a bar called Thee Klub, a small venue that did not have a liquor license and was only open two nights a week. Rebecca Rose (2019, p. 28) writes that middle- and upper-class white lesbians preferred private house parties to the few public spaces that did exist, which they perceived as controlled by gay men. DJ and organizer Chris Shepherd explains that Black lesbians and gay men like himself tended to patronize Black-oriented spaces and conceal their queerness. He recalls periodically visiting Thee Klub with some of his gay white male friends and says, "I don't remember ever seeing another Black person there."[12]

The situation in Halifax exemplifies challenges faced by lesbians and gays in smaller cities outside of major North American urban centers. For one thing, smaller populations meant fewer people to bring together under the banner of "lesbian and gay," and less chance of anonymity for those interested in doing so.[13] While larger cities in this era may have been able to sustain multiple dance spaces to serve lesbian and gay patrons, this did not seem possible in Halifax.[14] In the 1970s, Halifax was relatively isolated in terms of geography and demographics. The nearest major urban center is Montréal, Quebec, which is about

---

with public sex cultures that broke participants into smaller portions, obscuring the entirety so that "no one ever got to see the whole." He compares this to his first time visiting St. Mark's Bath as a young gay man in New York City in the early 1960s and seeing the massed bodies participating in homosexual acts illuminated for the first time. Seeing the sheer number of gay men convening at the baths transformed his understanding of the world: "what *this* experience said was that there was a population—not of individual homosexuals, some of whom I now and then encountered, or that those encounters could be human and fulfilling in their way—not of hundreds, not of thousands, but rather of millions of gay men, and that history had, actively and already, created for us whole galleries of institutions, good and bad, to accommodate our sex" (p. 293).

[12] C. Shephard (2018, July 12), interview by author.

[13] In 1976, the population of Halifax was just under 300,000; the population of Nova Scotia, the province of which Halifax is the capital, was just over double that amount. Compared to other cities that I analyze in this section, Halifax was relatively small. In 1976, for example, Toronto had about 4,800,000 residents and New York reported a population of nearly 7,500,000.

[14] This is not inherently productive or limiting to the development of the lesbian and gay liberation movement in the city. Fewer people also meant less of a chance of siloing off into smaller, separate lesbian and gay collectives demarcated by other factors of identity or political influence, which had both positive and negative consequences.

1,250 kilometers (or 775 miles) away. And while, as Will Straw (2022, p. 31) notes, *Billboard Magazine* named Montréal the second-best city in North America for disco culture in the 1970s (after New York City), a homosexual Haligonian could not simply take a bus or train to the larger, potentially gayer, city to get a feel for the scene through an exploratory meeting, dance, or drink – the bus to Montréal takes about twelve hours and the train nearly twice that. Considering its distance from other major North American cities, it's impressive how lesbian and gay activists in Halifax were able to actively participate in (and, in some cases, lead) national and international political actions. I describe the GAE's outsized role in the 1970s liberation politics in more detail later in this section because, like all the political formations I articulate, claiming space where gays and lesbians could dance together is what made subsequent political actions possible.

In January 1976, the GAE opened the doors to 1588 Barrington Street in Halifax's downtown core for their first dance. The building and the dance floor inside were referred to as "The Turret" because of the building's prominent spire. The first dance was hugely successful, both in raising funds for the GAE and in providing a space in which lesbian and gay people in Halifax could come together across forms of difference that previously kept the city's queer scene separate.[15] This dance served as the impetus for a significant political shift in Halifax, enabling a pluralistic notion of queerness that binds collective bliss with political action. This is not to suggest the forms of difference that previously kept these queer communities apart disappeared or became insignificant; on the contrary, The Turret became a space for difference to manifest and to challenge simplistic homogeneous notions of queerness. While Metcalfe tells me that the space was physically comfortable – "open, generous" – and served multiple purposes, he also makes clear that this was, at its core, a "contested space" that saw tense debates over its use, appearance, and purpose. Contrasting desires were most apparent in arguments over a mural painted by Rand Gaynor in the late 1970s and, years later, over the question of allowing men to dance shirtless, both of which were considered by some lesbians as evidence of sexism and misogyny within the organization. These examples of internal contestation are not signs of a failed political collective; they are precisely what makes the collective political.

---

[15] The building where the GAE found space to convene and dance is emblematic of early lesbian and gay liberation organizing in North America as the social movement initially cohered in physical space: other tenants included a health clinic aimed at youth and other underserved populations, an alternative recording studio, and more. Metcalfe tells me that The Turret building, throughout the 1970s and beyond, has been a space of heterogeneous connection: "queer communities, artistic communities, immigrant communities, the building has always been very generative." R. Metcalfe (2018, August 5), interview by author.

Metcalfe tells me that "we all just felt 'wow'! It really worked," as lesbians and gay men convened together on a dance floor framed by an association with gay and lesbian liberation. In the stories that Metcalfe and other GAE activists shared with me, it was apparent to attendees that The Turret was organized and managed by a lesbian and gay liberation collective, as the space was filled with political posters, banners, and murals. It was also clear because of how the dances were coordinated: members of the GAE worked the door, welcomed guests, directed them up the stairs to the dance floor and, before The Turret had adequate refrigeration, they would take turns climbing to the roof to get beer that was being chilled in the snow. The do-it-yourself atmosphere signaled to attendees that this venue was different from for-profit venues in the city: this was a space created by and for members of the lesbian and gay communities in Halifax. As many of the people I spoke with made clear, this made for a welcoming, warm, and accessible space – attendees knew they would be surrounded by other gay and lesbian people and that their own queerness would not be a liability or make them a target for harassment or surveillance as it might elsewhere.

The Turret accommodated a large dance floor and the building's spire provided space for a DJ booth (and a large collection of records) without separating the DJ from the dance floor. Shepherd, a regular DJ at The Turret in the late 1970s and early 1980s, explained to me that his philosophy was "P.A.R.T.Y! I would throw on a song and jump on the dance floor with everybody. Then rush back to the booth and do it again."[16] Within a few years of opening The Turret, Metcalfe (2014, pp. 29–30) writes, the GAE was "running a licensed lesbian and gay social venue ... open [six] nights a week" that made the GAE "*one of the wealthiest lesbian and gay organisations on the continent*" (italics added for emphasis) with gross revenues averaging a staggering "$300,000 to $600,000 annually." Archival records show that funds from dances enabled GAE members to connect with the broader liberation movement by travelling to other North American cities for conferences and events. The success of The Turret also meant that there were multiple secure employment opportunities for lesbians and gays in Halifax, fifteen years prior to the amendment of the Nova Scotia Human Rights Act that would include protection against employment discrimination based on sexual orientation.

In interviews, members of the GAE explained that the financial success of The Turret was hugely important for the group and its members. However, they all suggested that it was secondary to the dances' primary function: allowing

---

[16] C. Shephard (2018, July 12), interview by author.

participants to feel a sense of belonging and collective agency in the city – many for the first time. As GAE members explain all these years later, there is something unique about the way collective dance can make participants feel connected to others and part of something larger than themselves.

3.2 Sounds of Collectivity

While digging through the GAE's archival materials, I came across an undated, handwritten list of music that includes thirty-four songs from 1976, 1977, and a few from early 1978 (see Figure 5).[17] While the songs on this list vary in terms of genre (and modes of structure, tempo, rhythm, instrumentation, and vocal performance), the majority are bound together by the way they tap into the collectivizing sonics of dance music of the mid 1970s and the forms of collective intensity that the temporal arrangement of sounds encourage on the dance floor.

The sonic collectivity associated with disco music is audible in Rose Royce's 1976 song "Car Wash" – a song that appeared on the handwritten music request list and one that Shepherd remembers spinning often during GAE dances. In this song, we can hear disco music's collective ethos. For one thing, the sound of "Car Wash" is made possible by the collective labor of a large ensemble: electric guitar, bass guitar, drums, keyboards, congas or bongos, and several string instruments. Throughout the song, frequent and multiple handclaps and other forms of bodily percussion alongside a multiplicity of voices provide sonic support to the lead singer and emphasize the song's collectivity. These sonic signifiers do not just represent a music-making ensemble but also invite listeners and dancers into the musical collective. Participants on the dance floor do not need sheet music or rehearsals to sing and clap along; disco's participatory ethos are immediately recognizable, accessible, and inviting in this song.

"Car Wash" is also a good example of how disco music often subordinates the forward musical motion that is conventionally signaled through melody and pitch, while prioritizing groove and rhythm: while the song is complex and intricate in terms of rhythm, instrumentation, and repetition, chord changes that suggest forward motion are few and far between. By remaining on one chord for an extended amount of time, the musicians call attention to the musical present and, alongside them, listeners are invited to bask in the moment. This is not to suggest that melody, harmony, and pitch do not play integral roles in disco and

---

[17] I suspect that the document was written in mid 1978, because it includes "Disco Lucy," a disco version of the *I Love Lucy* theme song that was popular for a brief period before fading into obscurity in late 1978.

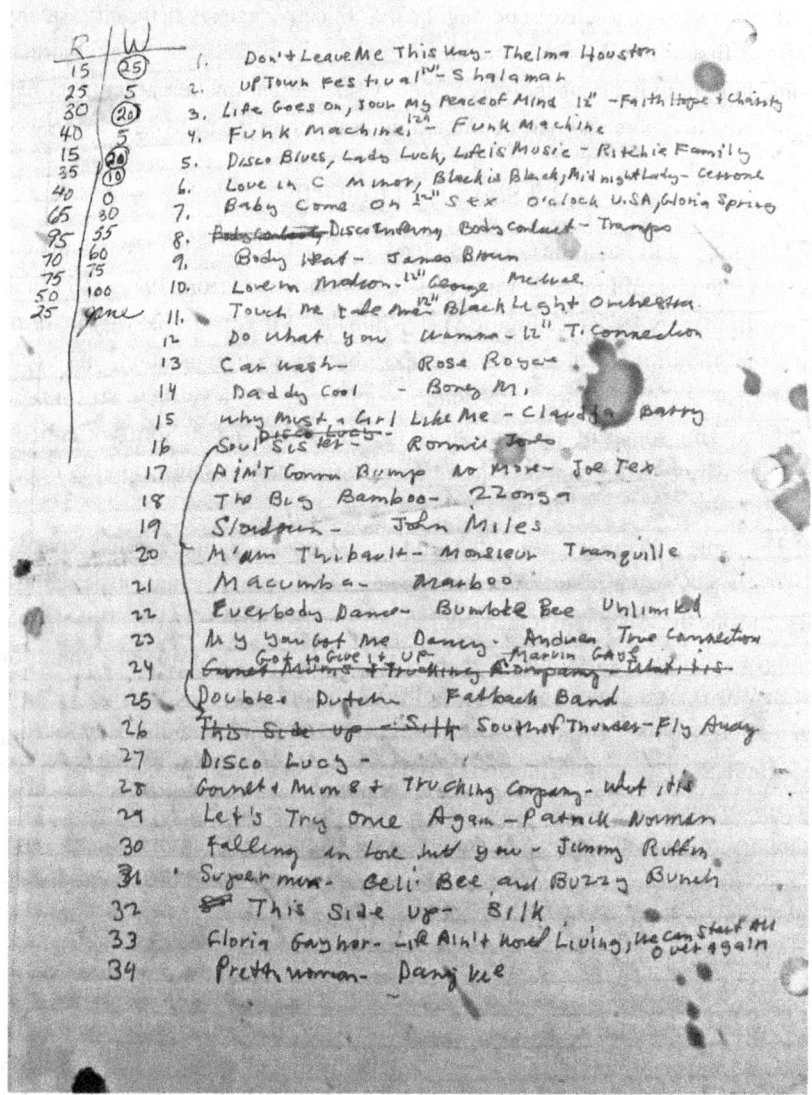

Figure 5 Handwritten list of music found in GAE's archival materials related to The Turret. Image appears courtesy of Robin Metcalfe.

subsequent dance music, just that dancers tend to be more attuned to other musical elements.

Another aspect of "Car Wash" that is particularly striking in its collectivizing effects is the way that the tempo fluctuates. At certain moments, the song speeds up and suggests a sense of immediacy and urgency, drawing listeners' attention to the present. When heard on a dance floor, this shift in tempo alters dancers' individual and collective sense of temporality. "Car Wash" is a particularly informative representation of the disco genre because the layering of rich instrumentation and the gradual building of musical tempo are maneuvers that disco DJs exhibit over a larger set of many songs to build collective intensity on the dance floor. Here, we experience these genre ideals in the space of one song. Breaks, crescendos, accelerandos, ritardandos – all of these playful shifts in musical conventions "encouraged crowds to express a form of liberationist energy as well as explore new forms of bodily movement, expression, sexuality, and desire" (Lawrence, 2022, pp. 308–309).

Tapping into the potential signaled by nonnormative aesthetic experience has long been a hallmark of lesbian and gay and, subsequently, queer politics. As many of the members of the GAE that I spoke with for this Element maintained, an aesthetic experience can, and regularly does, alter oneself and one's relationships. In the fall of 1976, for example, Shepherd organized a group to confront "fag bashers" throughout the city. A "number of us," he recalls, "had just gotten fed up with the whole gay bashing scene in the city ... We put the word out that anybody who was willing and able to stand up and have a fight ... let's get to it" (qtd. in Rose, 2019, p. 67). Shepherd, here, is a leader in the movement in part because of his skill as a DJ and his ability to create a sense of community and agency through musical sound. And his leadership role in the space of music participation translated into his leadership role in the community outside of The Turret. In other words, there is a thread of affective responses here that started on the dance floor: as a DJ, Shepherd made people feel good, feel their bodies, feel safe, and feel a sense of community and agency—and these ways of feeling carried over, beyond the dance floor.

In large and small cities in North America throughout the 1970s, dance enabled these visions of collective liberation. As Celeste Fraser Delgado and José Esteban Muñoz (1997, pp. 9–10) argue, by binding people in "rhythmic affinity ... dance incite[s] rebellions of everynight life." One particular example from New York City demonstrates how collective dance experiences can directly foment rebellion and political action: a particularly effective "zap" – a loud and disruptive political action – by the city's GAA in October 1971 harnessed dance floor collectivity and bliss for direct political activism.

3.3 Zapping New York

In his memoir, Arnie Kantrowitz (1977, p. 168) recounts multiple debates over the role of dances within the work of the GAA and the liberation movement more broadly. He writes that the GAA's aptly named "Pleasure Committee" steadfastly believed that "we could liberate our own heads and our sense of community at these dances, but the political people, believing we were diluting our purposes, accused the pleasure people of trying to 'dance their way to liberation.'" The factions – and the animosity that grew between them – "threatened to tear the fledgling organization apart." Fortunately, a specific night on the dance floor showed that collective social dance and direct political action are not antithetical; indeed, Kantrowitz (1977, p. 201) argues, GAA activists who were critical of dance quickly learned that they "could turn a dance into a new adventure and accomplish their civic mission with the same stroke."

Early on the morning of Sunday, October 3, 1971, the GAA's Firehouse on Wooster Street was packed with attendees of a regular Saturday night dance. A brief writeup in an October 1971 issue of *Gay Activist* notes that the dance was very well attended, and dancers were "in unusually high spirits" (Katz et al., 1971, p. 1). Buoyed by the collective intensity on the dance floor, a member of the GAA's Political Action Committee seized the DJ's microphone to tell the crowd about a problem facing New York City's gay and lesbian community: City Councilor Saul Sharison.

Sharison, the chairperson of the General Welfare Committee of the New York City Council, refused the GAA's frequent requests over the previous nine months to hold a hearing on a measure that would outlaw discrimination against gay people in both employment and housing. As luck would have it, the crowd of dancers was told, Sharison lived in a luxury condo a short walk from the GAA's Firehouse. At 2:30 a.m., after hours of dancing together, "hundreds of homosexuals left the Firehouse for [Sharison's] door-manned apartment building" and "woke the entire neighborhood with our anger" (Kantrowitz, 1977, p. 201–2). Sharison hadn't convened a meeting of the General Welfare Committee for over a year, but within weeks of the GAA's zap "the first public hearings on civil rights for homosexuals in New York City were under way" (Kantrowitz, 1977, p. 202). According to GAA member Marc Rubin (1999, n. p.), "no one who took part in that zap was left unchanged." This includes Sharison, whose neighbors organized to "have him evicted as an undesirable tenant" (Echols, 2010, p. 51).

I do not mean to suggest that the political force of dance floor sociality is only legitimate when it results in direct political actions like the GAE's gay community protection patrol in Halifax or the GAA's angry late-night march in New York City. These are exemplary moments in which collective dance directly leads to political actions that, in turn, directly lead to significant changes in local laws and the lived experiences of lesbian and gay individuals in the cities. Indeed, each serves as an extension of the community and agency already cultivated on the dance floor. As Ramón Rivera-Servera (2011, p. 259) writes, "my experience in the club not only allows me to feel desire, love, and community, but gives me the confidence and the knowledge to step proudly into other, more dangerous venues and seek, even demand, similar experiences from the world outside it." With respect to the aforementioned GAA members who were critical of the Pleasure Committee's commitment to collective dance, history has shown time and time again that we can indeed dance our way to liberation.

4 Collective Heat

Dance floors of the 1970s were well suited to engender a sense of collective belonging and imagination for lesbian and gay individuals. Steven F. Dansky (1970, p. 5) (the founder of Effeminism, a movement of profeminist men) describes dancing with friends, lovers, and strangers at gay community centers in New York City: our "dance is the ritual—an orgy of discharged energy—before we enter the struggle .... With acute aggressiveness we have encircled ourselves with protection against our oppressor." Kai Fikentscher (2000, p. 12) echoes Dansky's claim from an academic perspective, noting that underground dance spaces have served as "a type of cultural security zone for decades by three groups that have long been on the margins of society: African Americans, Latinos, and persons who describe themselves as either lesbian or gay." The sense of collectivity on a disco dance floor comes in part from what Fikentscher (2000, pp. 76, 79) calls dance music's "interactive performance" between DJs and dancers.

While dancers find ways to intervene in DJs' sets, they are also required to give up temporal control when they step onto a dance floor. Moving one's body to music that someone else selects and manipulates requires an openness: dancers must relinquish control of their embodied pace and sense of time, be open to shifts in timing, and allow their bodies to be animated in different ways. This temporal release encourages a sense of intimacy with DJs as well as with others on the dance floor – a site that allows participants to negotiate shared feelings of connection and pleasure. When Suzanne Cusick (2006, p. 74) asked, "what if music IS sex?" in the early 1990s, she identified ways that musical listening and sex both have the capacity to challenge seemingly fixed systems of gender, sexuality, and power. When we approach musical sound as a lover, she argues, it serves as "an active force that generates pleasure, that leads one body and soul into an alternate reality ... into intimacy" (Cusick, 2006, p. 74). Returning to Cusick's theory invites the question: if music is sex, is disco an orgy?

Dance music of the 1970s marked a profound shift in the history of popular music and collective dance. Disco and subsequent forms of social dancing that have been embraced by lesbian and gay collectives do not necessitate dance floor partnerships. As a result, they engender queer forms of dance floor community as methods through which individuals are welcomed into a larger collective body. While dancers may partner up on the dance floor, particularly if they are building an erotic connection with another individual, most dancers form larger groups. As Lawrence argues (2011, p. 235), earlier forms of social dance required partnerships, making dancers "internally focused" on their interaction with another individual. Disco dancing, however, revolves around its "status as a collective intensity" that "confirms its disruptive sexual intent." On the disco dance floor, dancers are not focused on themselves as part of a pair, but are instead focused on the broader, dynamic dance floor collective. Sasha Geffen (2020, p. 141) argues that this heterogeneous intensity is what made this historical moment so fruitful for collective queer politics. Describing David Mancuso's Loft, Geffen argues that "markers that distinguished individuals in the world outside ... seemed to soften and fall away within its walls. People were no longer differentiated and siloed, but part of something larger than themselves" through bodily expression to dance music.

Toronto-based DJ Deb Parent refers to this communal dynamism as "collective heat." She explains that "there are a few songs that are going to get people rushing onto the floor and the idea is to keep them there, build that energy, allow them to sweat and just be in their bodies. I think there is a collective heat for women particularly—there's a sensuality and a sexuality that happens on the dance floor." Part of this heat, she suggests, has to do with the way dance music encourages fleeting and shifting collective dancing bodies: "women are dancing with strangers ... [I'm] watching groups of women form and then unform, and then come together in a new shape—it's powerful as a DJ ... I feel like this is co-created, that we are in this together." For Parent, who has been an activist and DJ for decades, this experience on the dance floor is akin to other forms of activist work. She explains, "it's like Take Back the Night—a moment in time where women are safe and free where we can imagine if we could live all of our lives from this place without having to think through the danger or the consequences, without being told what we can or can't do, how we should or shouldn't dress, who we should or shouldn't love, all of that." As Parent illustrates, moments of collective heat on the dance floor allow participants to feel what is possible.[18]

For Fikentscher (2000, p. 57), there is an interdependent and "interactive performance" on post-1960s dance floors. For Lawrence there is a "collective intensity" and a "disruptive sexual intent." For Parent, there is a "collective

---

[18] D. Parent (2021, May 26), Interview by author.

heat" that simmers between dancers. What binds these perspectives together is a rather simple, but fundamentally important claim: dance music participation generates an intimate and powerful closeness with multiple others on the dance floor and allows individuals to feel as though they are part of a larger network of collective care (see Figure 6). Emphasizing shared experiences of bliss, these thinkers identify dance floors as sites of unbound possibility animated by erotic and intimate affinities. The dance floor can be a site of collective hope and shared dreams. Muñoz (2009, p. 9) argues that feelings of hope can be disappointed, but that "such disappointment needs to be risked if certain impasses are to be resisted." As he argues so convincingly, the promise of hope is less about the material conditions that it creates and more about the way hope's anticipatory illumination can reinvent our relationship to ourselves, to others, to everything we thought we knew. On the dance floor, surrounded by others, overwhelmed by bliss and an unfettered sense of what could be, everything can change.

Collective heat is often overlooked. Indeed, the tendency to think of moments of social formation and pleasure on the dance floor as a break from the real, difficult political work being done is a limiting perspective and regularly overlooks the exciting political potential of queer pasts. In all of the examples

Figure 6 Dancers at a Gay Community Dance Committee (GCDC) event in Toronto in the mid 1980s.
Photograph by Philip Share.

in this Element, it was dance music that enabled a capacious notion of queer political collectivity, altered participants' understanding of communal agency, and created an affective state that carried over into other political activities. In these histories, dance music was not secondary to political organizing – it was the spark that made political action seem necessary, doable, and desirable.

4.1 Contesting Community

The dance floor not only served as a site where lesbian and gay liberationists carved out space for difference in the broader heterosexual world, but also where they worked through internal political desires. A site of affiliation, contestation, and imagination, the dance floor was vital to the development of lesbian and gay liberation organizing in the 1970s and 1980s. I have shown that dance floor participation could produce, articulate, and represent how people understood themselves as gendered and sexual beings in the lesbian and gay liberation movement, but it also served as a site where participants could wrestle with notions of community and what lesbian and gay liberation could mean as a collective project.

In these histories, we can see the collective negotiation of community and political goals most clearly in relation to gender and race. This is not to say that up to this point, collective queer dance has been exclusively white and male. It never was, and it never could be. The dance floor was a productive site of liberation politics in the 1970s and 1980s precisely because it was a site where male supremacy and white supremacy could be challenged alongside heteronormativity. This challenge was inevitable because intersecting systems of oppression attempted to constrain the bodies, minds, and dreams of lesbian and gay individuals, and when one was scrutinized, others naturally followed.

The GLF's previously mentioned women's dance in New York City was brought to fruition, in part, because of luck and timing. As an organization committed to ending hierarchies and creating a truly collective process, the GLF pulled a name from a hat in January 1970 to choose their chair for the month. Jay's name was selected. In *Tales of the Lavender Menace*, Jay (1999, p. 126) writes that a women's dance was at the top of her list of priorities: "I hoped that by becoming the chair of the GLF, I could shape the dialogue so that there would be ... a women's dance. Many of the men resisted the idea of a separate event ... They might have seen it as the first sign of our independence—a step that would inevitably lead to our forming an autonomous group." Indeed, many published memoirs that chronicle participation in the early years of the GLF reference male members' trepidation around the idea of a women-only dance. In *The Gay Militants*, for example, Teal (1971, p. 58) quotes Ellen

Bedoz, who explained that "many men voiced strong objections" to the idea of a women's dance, worried that "the organization was splitting and ... that women would usurp GLF's allotted time at Alternate University for themselves without regard to men's needs."

Ultimately, the dance on April 3, 1970, was a resounding success – save for the violent thugs who appeared as volunteers were wrapping up. Bedoz (qtd. in Teal, 1971, p. 58) recalls that "what actually did happen was that not only did women continue to relate to GLF with a heightened sense of consciousness, but many new women were introduced to GLF through the dances." Jay (1999, p. 131) writes, "We started to have women's dances on a regular basis. Each dance drew more women." She quotes an anonymous writer published in *Rat* – a radical underground newspaper started in New York City in 1968 and reimagined as a women's liberation publication in 1970 – who argues that "Dancing with women is something else ... It was one of the most beautiful experiences of my life ... I am learning to love women, and the dance was a first step" (p. 129). As these women indicate, dance shaped the way they understood their lives and their place within the lesbian and gay liberation movement.

However, within the lesbian and gay liberation movements of the 1970s and 1980s, lesbian dancers and DJs had complicated terrain to navigate as even the most ostensibly radical social movements of the era replicated discriminatory logics. Many male activists in the gay liberation movement were uninterested in challenging the patriarchal norms that served them, in the same way that many women's liberation activists were unconcerned with the homophobic norms that they often replicated and benefitted from. In this context, lesbians and lesbian–feminists faced pressure from feminist separatists to not work with any men – even the super gay ones – as they simultaneously faced pressure from gay male liberationists to temper their critiques of patriarchy and male power. Lesbians and lesbian–feminists used music and dance to intervene in these broader political tensions and, in the process, shaped multiple movements of the era.

In her article "Dykes, Dancing, and Politics," Joyce Rock (1976, p. 17) critiques Toronto's lesbian liberation scene. As someone who arrived in Toronto only eight months before publishing the article, Rock reflects on how Toronto's lesbian culture compares to those in Montréal and New York City – two cities that had flourishing social scenes for lesbians in the 1970s. While lesbian–feminists may appear and convene for political actions in Toronto (including fundraising or benefit events), Rock is struck by how infrequently lesbians get together to "play" – to enjoy those experiences of simply being together as lesbians.

Rock (1976, p. 17) argues that "Forms of congregation—'playing,' if you will—are essential to the health of collectivity. They are also the fastest, most economical means by which you can gauge the community within which you find yourself." She contends that forms of play are particularly important for diverse political collectives because they provide contexts "where I may rub elbows with those whose energies and priorities are not identical to mine." As the title of Rock's article suggests, she believes that dancing is a particularly productive form of "play" for lesbian–feminists – a way in which women who love women can develop a more capacious understanding of community and possibilities for their lives. Ultimately, Rock (1976, p. 17) asks: "can those who don't *play* together *politique* together?"

Allen (2009, pp. 319–20) makes clear that this mixture of play and/as politics has long been a reality for those individuals who fall under the label of Black and queer: "From our positions—perched at the bar, twirling on the dance floor, shamelessly flirting, testing our sexual power—we easily found our way to parades and protests and letter writing and workshops and interventions and civil disobedience and consciousness-raising." Allen (2009, p. 320) argues that "for queers of colour," participating in play and politics "is not an either / or proposition, but a both / and." "Both / and" is a particularly compelling way of reframing the politics vs. pleasure binary that haunts lesbian and gay liberation histories. Critiques from Black lesbians and gays and from lesbian–feminists show that politics and pleasure can't be separated.

Dance floors were sites where Black dancers intervened in broader lesbian and gay political organizing. Indeed, as Allen (2009, p. 315) argues, dance spaces are primary sites where Black queer people imagine and build collectivity and better futures: "The club is the central institution of Black queer communion. Here we assert bodies, putatively dangerously riddled with disease and threat of violence, not only as instruments of pleasure but also as conduits to profound joy, and perhaps spiritual bliss and transcendent connection. Interstices or conduits that connect, perhaps to utopias." Here, Allen (2009, pp. 316–17) continues, "is a ground for, if not instantly coherent 'community,' certainly congregation, which suggests 'free your ass and your mind will follow'" – a space "in which there is the felt experience of common union, and a nurturing of individual projects and common experience."

I've previously made clear the indebtedness of lesbian and gay liberation dance histories – even those remembered as white – to African and Black musical ideals and genealogies. Indeed, the music called "disco" that was pushed by record labels across North America in the mid to late 1970s were "being recorded to accomplish what DJs in gay black clubs had done earlier" (Thomas, 1989, p. 29). Even when disco went mainstream at infamous clubs like Studio 54, Black dancers and DJs – and those who consciously followed their lead – built networks and sites where they could hold onto the promises of dance music that many considered paramount: bodily pleasure, heterogeneous collectivity, and complex musical rhythms that transport participants to a different psychological state. New York's Paradise Garage, a parking-garage-turned-dance club at 84 King Street that I discuss in greater detail in the next section, is one such venue that held on to the democratic and collective possibilities of dance. According to Michael Paoletta (2000, p. 54), "the Garage placed the spotlight firmly where it belonged: on the entire dance floor experience ... unlike the trendier uptown clubs, the downtown Garage didn't discriminate based on skin color, sexuality, or sexual preference." Part of what made Paradise Garage such a transformative experience for attendees, according to Arnaldo Cruz-Malavé (2007, p. 81), is that – unlike many gay discos that "by 1981 had become increasingly racially and culturally homogeneous and middle-class" – the Garage was "racially and culturally mixed." On Saturday nights, heterogeneous queer collectives convened on the dance floor and enacted a better world. Importantly, sexual pleasure was fundamental to musical experience at Paradise Garage: *Village Voice* columnist Michael Musto tells Cathy Che (2001, p. 56) that "Paradise Garage's DJ Larry Levin would send the crowd into orgasms on the dance floor. People literally got off dancing, which was an ecstatic experience there in and of itself."

Throughout the 1970s, collective lesbian and gay social dance allowed participants to experience a sense of open and unbound possibility that illuminated the limitations of the present. This hopeful sense of collective potential became increasingly difficult (and important) to hold on to in the following decade. The 1980s saw a variety of challenges that would fundamentally shape the lives of lesbian and gay politics and dance floor collectives. The authors of *No Turning Back: Lesbian and Gay Liberation for the '80s* (Goodman, 1983, p. 1) open their book by writing that "[w]e are facing a time of turbulence and difficulty. A well-organized move from the right is seeking to erase the civil rights gains of the past decade." It's going to be a difficult few years, the authors suggest. From our current vantage point, we know that what was to come was worse than anyone could have possibly imagined.

4.2 Dark Days Ahead

Neoliberal ideologies solidified in the early 1980s with market-oriented policies of deregulation, privatization, and austerity and curtailed the burgeoning social movements of the 1970s. Women's liberation, gay liberation, Black feminist organizing, Black power politics, labor activism, and anti-imperialist movements promised new beginnings and alternative visions of the future. However, right-wing political gains systematically dismantled the revolutionary momentum that once seemed capable of changing the world – rending the 1980s a "denouement" of social change (Duggan, 2003, p. ix) and a time of "revolutionary disappointment" (Allen, 2021, p. 120).

The logics and systems of neoliberalism led to rapid gentrification in urban spaces around North America in the 1980s, around the same time the AIDS epidemic began. Gentrification had a profound effect on more than just the physical spaces of urban centers like New York City: gentrification is also a process that works on the mind – the imagination – and the spirit of a space and those living there, most notably through the elimination of difference (Schulman, 2012). Neoliberalism, gentrification, and the AIDS crisis combined to destroy spaces where lesbians and gay men could find collective bodily pleasure and provided conservative cultural critics fodder to close spaces that enabled gay sexual experiences in New York City (Delany, 1999). During the AIDS crisis, such spaces were prime targets of urban cleanup campaigns across North America.

Following the first decades of the AIDS crisis, the LGBTQ2+ community engaged in a process of collective forgetting – what Christopher Castiglia and Christopher Reed (2011, p. 9) call "unremembering" and "temporal isolation" – in an effort to distance the community from a generation stigmatized as sexually promiscuous, excessive, and licentious and pursue mainstream or homonormative belonging and acceptance. Narratives of normativity and respectability in the present and past, Roderick A. Ferguson (qtd. in Dinshaw et. al., 2007, p. 193) reminds us, are often thinly veiled "attempts to close off prior critical and sexual universes" and limit what seems possible in the present. They are also detrimental to our ability to imagine alternative possibilities for the future.

The AIDS epidemic attacked many of the sexual possibilities that are fundamental to lesbian and gay culture; Douglas Crimp (2004, p. 140) famously argues that "alongside the dismal toll of death, what many of us have lost is a culture of sexual possibility: back rooms, tea rooms, bookstores, movie houses, and baths; the trucks, the pier, the ramble, the dunes." Years earlier, in a June 1983 article in the *New York Native*, Denneny (2023, pp. 137–38) captured what was on the line for lesbian and gay liberation in early years of the AIDS epidemic:

> Today the gay world is facing an outbreak of history, one of those rare moments in time when things can actually change in a fundamental way ... AIDS could destroy the gay community, not through killing each and every one of us, but by attacking our deepest values, which concern sex, and by isolating us into homosexual monogamy. Of course, homosexuals would still exist—isolated and dispersed among the straight population, leading private monogamous lives—but the gay *community* would disappear.

Gay community, in Denneny's thinking, is built on physical contact, intimate connection, and sexual possibility. But in the 1980s, spaces that facilitated such experiences faced attacks on multiple fronts: neoliberal ideals and economic policies meant that previously affordable spaces became increasingly inaccessible and eroded the ability for activists, artists, and dreamers to spend time building political movements and alternatives instead of being productive under capitalism. At the same time, the AIDS epidemic (and the refusal of people in power to do anything about it) decimated lesbian and gay communities through illness, death and – for the lucky ones – exhaustion.

The AIDS epidemic of the 1980s radically reshaped lesbian and gay collectives in North America. Activism in this era brought lesbians and gay men together in ways that were both personally and politically transformative (see, for example, Cvetkovich, 2003; Faderman, 1991; and Sullivan, 2022). The 1980s afforded new possibilities for queer Black communities. Contrary to Lisa Duggan's (2003) argument that the 1980s was largely a "denoument" of social change, Allen (2021, p. 8) argues that the 1980s was the decade when "[f]olks first began to dance, fuck, organize, and make art under the banner of 'Black gay'" – an identity and ideal that emerged "directly out of the political, artistic, and activist work of radical Black lesbians of the 1970s." Dance spaces were fundamental to the decade's broader shifts, serving as sites where individuals could contribute to broader social political projects and transformations and intervene in a world ravaged by AIDS.

5 Disease on the Dance Floor

In the early years of the AIDS epidemic, collective dance took on additional significance for those committed to the ideals of lesbian and gay liberation. In the face of government inaction, regular people had to become medical experts, caregivers, fundraisers, developers of educational materials, and more. Because dance floors had already been established within the community as productive sites for political organizing, they were privileged during the early years of AIDS as sites where people assembled, where participants were open to being with and learning from others, and where bodily possibilities and intimacy were at the forefront. For many people, participating in gay and lesbian collective dance in the 1980s served as an embodied form of consciousness-raising through which they gained entry into a political collective navigating a treacherous reality – a lifeline when they needed it most.

During the early years of the AIDS crisis, however, dance spaces took on a new sheen of suspicion and fear for many participants. While the danger of police violence and the ever-present possibility of bashing from fellow citizens – hallmarks of lesbian and gay social venues in urban spaces – continued to cast a shadow over queer collective experiences, the early 1980s ushered in an even more terrifying threat: an unfamiliar and rapidly spreading virus that seemed to target gay men. Like other venues that enabled embodied and erotic queer experiences – bathhouses, bars, and similar spaces for cruising and physical contact – dance spaces in the early 1980s were quickly framed by politicians, public health officials, and even lesbian and gay people themselves as dangerous sites where the virus was being spread.

At the same time, community dance spaces allowed lesbian and gay activists to work through complex feelings sparked by illness, death, and brutal manifestations of governmental inaction and disinterest. Most importantly, dance floors served as an effective training ground for activists by allowing them to perceive alternatives to the harsh realities of life. Many of the activists I spoke with explained that, even in dark times, glimpsing what was possible and gaining access to feelings of collective joy had the capacity to reframe the suspicion and terror that permeated gay life in the first few years of the epidemic. During this time, the dance floor connected participants with a history of queer resilience and survival and allowed them to express feelings of despair alongside others whose lives were profoundly restructured by the ongoing crisis.

The poster in Figure 7 announces a benefit dance at Paradise Garage on Thursday, April 8, 1982. The upper and largest section of the poster features a pencil-drawn, headless male figure. The perspective is from below, so viewers look upward at his crotch where the bulge of his penis pushes against his tight Speedo-style shorts. He appears to hold an umbrella in his left hand and something less obvious in his right hand – might it be the end of a hose? Whatever it is, it resembles a flaccid penis. The figure grips both hands tightly and the veins in his arms pop. In the middle section of the poster, "SHOWERS" is written in large red letters. Matching red frames border the image of the man and the event details in the bottom section: the location and time of the dance, what attendees can expect, and where they can get tickets. The text notes that Showers is a fundraising benefit dance hosted by the Gay Men's Health Crisis (GMHC) "to aid gay men with Kaposi's sarcoma and other gay related immunodeficiencies." This dance was the first public event organized by the newly formed GMHC, a New York-based group of volunteers "founded to define AIDS and contain its effects" (Kayal, 1993, p. 1), though at the time of its formation and the Showers dance party, the term "AIDS" did not yet exist. That night at Paradise Garage, the GMHC raised over $50,000 to provide financial and medical support for gay men in New York City who were falling ill with the new, unnamed, and terrifying disease.

Figure 7 A poster for April Showers at Paradise Garage on April 8, 1982. Manuscript and Archives Division, New York Public Library. Courtesy of the Gay Men's Health Crisis (GMHC).

Paradise Garage was well suited for this type of event: it featured a variety of lounges surrounding a large, open dance floor with perhaps one of the most impressive sound systems produced in the 1970s. It was also colloquially known as "Paradise Gay-Rage" because, according to Ivan L. Munuera (2020, p. 133), "the queer community that frequented the club was extremely politically active" and angry about the oppressive conditions under which they lived. Peter Shapiro (2005, pp. 261–63) argues that Paradise Garage is "considered by many to be the greatest discotheque ever" and "probably the only nightclub ever to be constructed for a specific DJ." Larry Levan, a Black gay dance music legend who developed a genre of music that would subsequently be named "garage," had a decade-long DJ residency at the venue. While Levan's mastery in the DJ booth was a prime draw to Paradise Garage, so too was the community Levan drew. A private club that welcomed members, their guests, and out-of-towners who showed identification that proved they lived elsewhere, Paradise Garage had a majority Black and Latinx clientele that was committed to dancing. An unnamed informant featured in the 2003 dance music documentary *Maestro* explains that dancing at Paradise Garage was "about completely being safe from the social restrictions of the outside. Everything that the moral majority told you you couldn't do, it didn't exist anymore." This sense of freedom was not the only way that the Garage held on to the spirit and promise of earlier lesbian and gay dance floors. By the early 1980s, the gay dance scene of New York City was becoming more and more segregated based on gender, race, and class. Cruz-Malavé (2007, p. 82) argues that "[i]n clubs such as the Flamingo, and the ultimate gay male disco, the Saint, which had opened in 1980 in the East Village ... the patrons were almost exclusively white and male, and the environment seemed thoroughly engineered to produce a sense of communal belonging through the isolation and exaltation of their patrons' visual commonality." In the context of increasing segregation and categorization based on visual markers, Paradise Garage's emphasis on community through musical sound – as well as its "racial, ethnic, social, and sexual mix" (Cruz-Malavé, 2007, p. 83) – made it a pivotal space for burgeoning queer collectives responding to the AIDS epidemic.

The looming threat of the new illness was palpable on the dance floor of Paradise Garage during the Showers event in April 1982. This dance was DJ'd not by Levan, but by Francois Kevorkian. Michael VerMeulen (1982, p. 62), who wrote about Showers in his 1982 article "The Gay Plague," noted that "the evening proved a substantial success and a coming together of many disparate cliques within the New York gay scene. More than 2,000 men, and a few women, too, paid $20 apiece to walk up the ramp and dance against disease." He wrote that GMHC President Paul Popham made a short statement when

Kevorkian cut the dance music, saying, "we are in the grip of a medical emergency," something "has brought us closer to death." Kevorkian recalls that throughout the event, people would grab the microphone and say things like, "this is an emergency, people are dying left and right" (qtd. in Lawrence 2004, p. 328). According to Munuera (2020, pp. 135–36), the cries coming from the dance floor that April night in 1982 were prophetic, as "a significant percentage of the people who attended the party succumbed to the epidemic in the years following, including Michael Brody, the proprietor of Paradise Garage; Paul Popham, one of the founders of GMHC; Keith Haring, the artist behind the graffiti that decorated the club; and Larry Levan."

White served on the executive committee of the GMHC and briefly volunteered as the president of the organization before moving aside to let Popham take over. White (2009, p. 287) looks back on the Showers dance party as an error in judgement: we "made lots of mistakes. Instead of instantly enlisting the help of the federal government, we organized a disco fund-raiser. We thought small ... We didn't understand that we were watching the beginnings of an epidemic that would soon enough infect forty million people worldwide." In hindsight, White's regret is understandable. Although, as he writes, "no one else had that sort of apocalyptic prescience any more than we did" (p. 287). Further, his suggestion of turning to the federal government for assistance in April 1982 strikes me as specious. Ronald Reagan, who was elected president of the United States in 1981, was famously apathetic about the disease; he didn't even utter the term "AIDS" until 1985. Munuera (2020, pp. 133, 136), however, presents a contrasting view of Showers, arguing that the fundraiser was an important intervention in the early years of the AIDS epidemic. "In the confusion of the early 1980s, when AIDS was still an unknown medical affliction," he argues, "Paradise Garage provided spaces for information and collective discussion." Indeed, he continues, "what happened in New York's nightclubs had a series of wide-ranging ramifications throughout the city." If we refuse to recognize the political possibilities of dance floors in the lesbian and gay liberation era and the early years of the AIDS epidemic – if we disavow the promise of sweaty bodies consolidated through musical sound and the shared desire for something better – we'll never adequately understand the past, the present, and our potential futures. Death and life, bliss and misery; the dance floor was the site.

5.1 Dance and Despair

The title of an article by Lawrence K. Altman that appeared in the *New York Times* on July 3, 1981, declared, "Rare Cancer Seen in 41 Homosexuals." A month prior, the US government's *Morbidity and Mortality Weekly Report* described five "young men, all active homosexuals," who exhibited a confusing mix of multiple infections. When these reports were published in the summer of 1981, the bizarre condition being described did not yet have a name. Over the next twelve months, it would be named a "gay plague," Gay Related Immune Deficiency (GRID), and Acquired Community Immune Deficiency Syndrome (ACIDS) by medical professionals, politicians, and activists. Randy Shilts (1987) contends that individuals associated with specific lesbian and gay communities in New York and Toronto colloquially referred to the virus as "Saint's Disease" in reference to the popular gay nightclub in New York City where many of the fit young men on the dance floor were falling ill. Eventually, in the summer of 1982, a new name for the virus was proposed at a medical conference in Washington: Acquired Immune Deficiency Syndrome (AIDS).

In 1982, little was known about the causes, effects, and proliferation of the virus. Lesbian and gay individuals – and people who loved them – searched for information that could help them make sense of the illness and find methods of protection. Much of the information that circulated in the early to mid 1980s was conjectural. According to Bill Lewis (1982, p. 38), a Toronto-based scientist and contributor to *The Body Politic*, "everything gay men did that straight men didn't was dragged forth as a possible cause. Abundant sex, poppers, fisting, drugs, ingestion of too much sperm, staying up too late—all have been put forward as an explanation." Tim McCaskell (2016, p. 171) writes that "although those with connections to New York, like [Michael] Lynch and [Bill] Lewis, seemed more preoccupied, the general message in Toronto was that this was just more anti-gay hysteria. There was still only one known case of [Kaposi's sarcoma] in Canada, and U.S. politics seemed more threatening than a gay-targeted epidemic."

AIDS-influenced homophobia was compounded by profound economic inequality in the 1980s and many politicians and ostensible medical experts were quick to blame gay men's sexual culture for the development and rapid spread of AIDS. Cindy Patton (1985, p. 69) notes that right-wing politicians regularly argued that "any money spent on AIDS [prevention] was too much, that AIDS was an elective disease created by homosexuals who might just as well die off." Throughout the early 1980s, it became painfully clear that the communities most directly affected by the disease couldn't turn to governmental entities to save them – they would need to save themselves. Many took up the mantle: activists became amateur primary care specialists, ad-hoc care collectives, and health researchers chasing new theories on causes, effects, and potential treatments for the disease. Exhausted, grief-stricken, and up against a seemingly insurmountable challenge, these activists faced a "deafening silence" (Gould 2009, p. 11) that marked the first years of the AIDS crisis.

Maria Murphy (2018, p. 38) argues that this silence was, at times, "punctuated by laughter." When the illness was raised in White House press briefings between 1982 and 1985, she explains, Deputy White House Press Secretary Larry Speakes laughed off the reporters' concerns and regularly teased them for showing interest in a disease that seemed to directly target gay men. During these years, when the White House responded to questions about the AIDS crisis with laughter, there were thousands AIDS-related deaths in the United States accordingly to the Center for Disease Control (CDC).

Dancing in the early years of the AIDS epidemic was complicated. For some people, returning to dance floors where they had previously found joy with friends and lovers who had died was somber and unappealing. As Echols (2010, pp. 151–52) writes, "when AIDS began decimating communities of men who had danced together and loved together, sometimes for more than a decade, it was horrifying and terrifying. As the casualties mounted, the loss and grief were almost too much to bear." Toronto-based organizer Chris Lea told me something similar, remembering that "people were just dying so quickly and nobody really felt like dancing."[19]

Throughout the 1980s, the numbers of dancers on many established lesbian and gay dance floors in urban spaces dwindled significantly. There are multiple reasons for this decline, all of them having to do with AIDS: many people died from the disease and many others were exhausted from caregiving responsibilities and from burying their friends and lovers. Ed Jackson, a founder of the AIDS Committee of Toronto (ACT) explains that "AIDS had ravaged the community—especially the gay male community that filled the dance floors. People were tired." Additionally, he notes, the majority of activist energies and fundraising attention went toward AIDS causes throughout the 1980s: "We focused on AIDS and other organizations got left behind; they had a lot of trouble competing because AIDS was so overwhelming."[20] For volunteer-run organizations, AIDS meant that volunteer numbers plummeted.

For many queer individuals in the 1980s, AIDS was overwhelming on a broad social level – an apocalyptic and existential threat to the idea of gay life and gay liberation – but also as an immediate material danger in the everyday. Matthew J. Jones (2017, p. 188) argues that "an HIV/AIDS diagnosis brought with it new temporal flows" for sick individuals and those who loved them. Even for long-term survivors, he writes, "sick days, doctor's visits, hospitalization, unemployment, funerals, sick friends, time spent haggling with insurance companies and hospitals, and participation in clinical trials or

---

[19] C. Lea (2021, May 21), interview by author.
[20] E. Jackson (2021, May 12), interview by author.

activism wrenched the gears of daily life." The temporal structure of everyday life was transformed by AIDS, even for those who did not personally contract the disease, because its effects were so pervasive and required profound forms of collective care.

Jones's description of the "new temporal flows" brought on by the AIDS epidemic points toward the political function of dance floor experience in the 1980s. While many people stopped dancing, lesbian and gay dance parties continued and, for many participants who remained on dance floors, served to disrupt the flow of life structured by AIDS. A break in these temporal currents didn't mean escaping from the social reality bounded by AIDS, but for many it offered a way to return to their body, to be among others whose lives were also framed by the disease, and to perceive the continued strength of the communities of which they were a part. As I have argued previously, music's temporal nature makes it a particularly effective method for intervening in and reconstructing experiences of time. Garcia-Mispireta (2023, p. 13) argues that music's capacity to "play with expectation, anticipation, and synchronicity" is what makes collective musical experiences so promising: "since music unfolds in time ... it seems especially well suited to convey the expectant qualities [Ernst] Bloch associates with hope and utopia."

Indeed, many gay and lesbian people held on tightly to the dance floor as a site where they could feel bliss and pleasure even from within the brutal reality of the AIDS epidemic. For Alan Miller, "dances offered some relief" from the brutality of the everyday. He explained to me that "everything else was just falling apart around us" and dances offered a moment of collective joy that was hard to find elsewhere. Miller's partner Gram Campbell died on January 17, 1990; they had been together for almost nine years and although "Gram didn't always feel like dancing," they would often go out, find a secluded corner of the venue, and dance the night away together. Miller remembers going dancing in the years after Gram died, to force himself to get out of the house and spend time with friends, but also to remember the times he and Gram danced together. "These dances kept me going," he explains.[21]

5.2 Kinship and Care

Describing the feelings of bliss and belonging on the dance floor, Allen (2009, p. 316–18) writes:

> Emile Durkheim might call this form of sociality *collective effervescence,* rituals of assembly wherein groups author and reauthor themselves through exuberant collective practices. Victor Turner would call this liminal space in

---

[21] A. Miller (2021, April 15), interview by author.

which newly imagined perspectives unfaithful to the status quo emerge, *communitas* ... here the in-between spaces we occupy feel less lonely, individualized, and vulnerable ... The transformation takes place through collective effervescence evoked by the music, the people, and the safe*r* space for spinning and spiraling. This may be only for the moment.

For some people, collective dance was also a method through which they could work through difficult feelings, be it rage at governmental bodies or the circumstances of the world more broadly. David Roman (2011, p. 305) writes that dancing during the height of the AIDS epidemic "connected me with a history of queer resilience, a kind of reenergizing necessary to get through the week. But mainly ... dance was a way to express my anger and feelings of despair brought on by the relentless death toll I was witnessing." In a historical moment brimming with AIDS-related panic, stigma, and homophobia, many gay men felt compelled to hide their queerness in their everyday lives. As Lawrence (2016, p. 436) argues, dance venues that "celebrated gay identity as something positive, even during negative times" served as a lifeline for many people.

For many people, the effect of feeling good on the dance floor sustained them long after they left the venue. Brent Nicholson Earle, whose activism brought attention to the plight of living with AIDS and the need for education and prevention efforts, suggests that his experiences on gay dance floors were foundational to his activism: "[b]eing at the Saint," he explains to Lawrence (2016, p. 437), "being part of a tribe, being part of this glorious community, went hand-in-hand with my becoming an AIDS activist ... I would never have dreamt I could become a hero if I hadn't had that image of transcendent glory, that iconized version of myself, bestowed to me under the dome of the Saint." For many dancers, experiences of bliss and *communitas* on the dance floor readied them for battle elsewhere.

Like bathhouses and bars, dance venues served as sites where individuals could access rapidly changing information about the disease. Promotion in mainstream publications or in public spaces such as on billboards or public transit was prohibitively expensive for most community organizations. Accordingly, these groups had to find inventive ways to reach their intended audiences and disseminate important information. In the early years of AIDS, dances had additional functions in the lesbian and gay liberation movement: they simultaneously raised funds to support the work of AIDS organizations while convening the population with whom these groups needed to communicate.

The Gay Community Dance Committee (GCDC), a Toronto-based community coalition, was formed in 1981 with a simple aim: to encourage collaborations among independent gay and lesbian organizations in Toronto and surrounding areas to host dances that would be larger than what any individual organization could hold on their own. Participating groups would sell tickets, provide volunteer labor for necessary duties at each dance, and split the profits. A core management group would take care of all other preparations and arrangements. Lesbian and gay community groups signed on in droves.[22] Funds raised at dances were distributed among participating groups based on two factors: ticket sales and volunteer hours provided. During the 1980s, the GCDC's dance floor was a primary source of funding for lesbian and gay liberation in Toronto. A conservative estimate of the funds raised by the GCDC over their nearly twelve-year-long tenure is just over $250,000. But like all the examples I articulate in this Element, the impact of these dances is much broader and more important than their financial successes. What makes these historical dance floors remarkable is the way that they provoke a sense of communal care and kinship that transforms participants and reanimates the world in which they live.

GCDC organizer Rob Stout remembers AIDS organizations distributing pamphlets at dances in the 1980s that included current research on the disease. Many of these pamphlets were designed and produced by the AIDS Committee of Toronto (ACT), a group formed by lesbian and gay activists in 1983 to provide leadership on the issue of AIDS that became a trusted source of information about AIDS in Toronto and Canada more broadly. This had to do, in part, with the language that they used in their educational material – precise and straightforward sexual language that Toronto Public Health often shied away from. It also had to do with the fact that members of ACT were situated in the communities that they wanted to serve. Many of the founding members of ACT were involved in the GCDC since its beginning. These were not public health officials at a remove from the community – these were fellow activists, fellow dancers.

Jackson recalls the difficulty of getting current and reliable information on the virus to community members, noting that "we always used bars and baths as major outlets to reach people—we saw queer social events as major sites of information dissemination." The materials distributed at GCDC dances and other social venues around the city outlined services for people living with the virus, information for caregivers, and more. Jackson explains that materials distributed to dance attendees would explain safer sex practices and, in later years, would make important "distinctions between anal and oral sex based on

---

[22] Participating groups included the ACT, Canadian Gay Archives, Gay Asians of Toronto, Gay Community Appeal, Gays and Lesbians Against the Right Everywhere, Lesbian and Gay Youth Toronto, Lesbian Mothers' Defence Fund, the Right to Privacy Committee, Zami, and many more.

the science ... as opposed to saying that all sex was equally risky." Pamphlets would also promote condom use and provide up-to-date information on testing.[23]

That GCDC dances attracted attendees from surrounding regions was also an important factor in disseminating information about participating groups, community priorities, and AIDS. For some gays and lesbians, GCDC dances were their only interactions with a broader community that included networks of activists and health service organizations. The educational aspect of these dances is significant: individuals would convene on the dance floor and feel a sense of collective belonging. When they left the dance floor, the effects of these experiences travelled with them to different regions. Disseminating educational materials at GCDC dances was a way to spread this information to individuals from multiple geographic and social communities.

While ACT was widely perceived as producing important and potentially life-saving educational materials, Jackson notes that accessing stable government funding was difficult. As a result, he explains, "fundraising was always a major problem." At GCDC dances, where profits were distributed among participating groups based on ticket sales and the volunteer labor hours they provided, the AIDS crisis encouraged more fluid ways of understanding associations and allegiances. Ron Merko remembers that People With AIDS (PWA) organizations in Toronto had trouble building a volunteer base to work the dances and, as a result, many people who joined the GCDC through different community organizations would often shift their organizational affiliations to donate their volunteer credits to PWA groups (see Figure 8). Volunteers with Lesbian and Gay Youth Toronto, a participating group with a large volunteer base, frequently donated their credits to PWA organizations in the mid and late 1980s, demonstrating the possibility of affiliative political coalition across difference.[24]

The way GCDC members shifted affiliations to support pressing political and social issues of the moment exhibits a type of collective politics and community caregiving that took place during the early years of the AIDS epidemic. So too does this type of community support mimic the embodied experiences that make dance floors so generative for collective formation and belonging: fleeting moments of embodied connection enable new ways of understanding one's relations, and these experiences of togetherness contain structures of feeling that outlast the moment of connection. The AIDS epidemic intensified awareness of the ephemeral nature of connection and feelings of belonging.

---

[23] E. Jackson (2021, May 12), interview by author.
[24] R. Merko (2021, June 20), interview by author.

Figure 8 Dancers at a GCDC event in the late 1980s.
Photograph by Philip Share.

According to Patton (1985, p. 16), the persistent threat of AIDS meant building a "community with people who could be dead in two months." Jack Halberstam (2005, p. 2) argues that queer time "emerges most spectacularly" during the AIDS epidemic, as the "constantly diminishing future creates a new emphasis on the here, the present, the now, and while the threat of no future hovers overhead like a storm cloud, the urgency of being also expands the potential of the moment and ... squeezes new possibilities out of the time at hand."

Allen (2009, p. 317) argues that the dance floor is a space "in which there is the felt experience of a common union, and a nurturing of individual projects and common experience." This doesn't mean that differences of identity and desire between dancers are erased, but that shared experiences of music, rhythm, and movement ascend and take precedence. When situated as a temporary collective made through musical sound and bodily orientation to that sound, dancers can more readily recognize shared priorities and the ways that the shared desires of the dance floor community diverge from dominant logics and ideologies. In the early years of the AIDS epidemic, Munuera (2020, pp. 137–38) argues, dancers shared "an understanding of their relationship with HIV and AIDS different from one embraced by medical authorities, media, and government officials," and a kinship "across class and race differences with intersecting concerns: what it meant to live with HIV and AIDS." Alternative ways of understanding ourselves and others surface and take shape on the dance floor. At a time of profound threats to queer ways of life, such alternatives – and their value – become easier to perceive and more compelling.

Dance floor kinship offers an opportunity to reorient ourselves to different pasts, presents, and futures. An orientation toward queer pasts and their potential is perhaps more important now than ever before. In his collection of poetry *These Waves of Dying Friends: Poems*, Michael Lynch (1989, p. 6) writes of "the telling mark" of great DJs who can create seamless, seemingly everlasting mixes of music that "don't conclude but do go round again / one more time." For Lynch, a Toronto-based academic and activist, this everlasting presentness grants him access to dance floor temporality that gives him the sense "of nothing ended, nothing altered, nothing new / in the only life I count as true: the dancefloor." "Last night," he continues (1989, p. 6), "I danced as we did two years ago / Alive with life, with Larry, Vito / Ray and a dozen unnamed others / the virus thinks it has taken from the floor." Those who died from AIDS, Lynch's poem suggests, remain part of the everlasting dancing collective because stepping onto the dance floor is akin to stepping into a broader, imagined collective in an alternate space and time.

6 Conclusion: We Should Be Dancing

> Much has happened as time stood still—while we conjured moments of rapturous faggotry.
>
> — Jafari S. Allen (2009, p. 312)

It's 2023. I've been to this venue before, so I know where I'm headed even though there's no signage to indicate the entrance. I walk down the alley and see the purple door under the black metal staircase. I pull my phone from my pocket and take a photo of the entryway. In a giddy haze amplified by a few gin and sodas, the photo on my screen recalls for me a series of postcards that were published in *Fireweed: A Feminist Quarterly* in 1982: simple photographs of unassuming building doors in Montréal, Vancouver, and Toronto that subtly signaled entryways to underground lesbian dance venues (see Figures 9, 10, and 11). I send the photo to a group text thread and write: "If you listen closely, you can hear dance music coming from below. Just follow the sound!" Within seconds, a friend texts back: "omfg. Okay, Dorothy, will do."

I open the door and start down the steep, narrow staircase to the windowless underground gallery that – for one night – is reimagined as a gay bar by the artist collective QSO that promoted the event with the motto "This Space Does Not Exist." They're making a statement about the constructed nature of the event, but also provoking that shared impulse among queers who crave something else, something more: we'll search until we find what was promised or we'll find each other and manifest something better.

Figure 9 Postcard of The Cameo Club, Toronto, ON, published in *Fireweed*, 1982. Photograph by Molly Counts. Postcard design by Susan Sturman.

Figure 10 Postcard of The Quadra, Vancouver, BC, published in *Fireweed*, 1982. Photograph by Allison Sawyer. Postcard design by Susan Sturman.

When I reach the basement, I walk to the bar and order a drink. The bar is covered in wheat-pasted reproductions of queer event posters from the past five decades, layered and mixed in a messy pseudo-chronology, fusing the events and their eras into a composite of historical happenings. At the time of their production, these posters anticipated the future: "Gay Dance! This Saturday!" announces one from 1975. Now the posters – some ripped and partial – reference opportunities for collective queer sociality that are situated in the past. All I can discern from some

Figure 11 Photograph of the plumb, Toronto, ON, 2023. Photograph by Craig Jennex.

fragments in the collage is that something else was once there. *Something else was once here.* The layered presentation of these materials points to the unfinished nature of the project that is queer sociality: messy innovation, destructive promise, burgeoning revolutions, and irrepressible dreams. Ahmed (2017, p. 16) argues that "citations can be feminist bricks: they are the materials through which, from which, we create our dwellings." Tonight, this idea is actualized as queer historical ephemera cover and fortify this space of embodied and erotic potential.

I turn from the bar and walk toward the source of the music. A neon light twisted into the shape of the word "utopia" hangs on the far wall. *A warm illumination on the horizon*, I think to myself, comforted by the fact that José still haunts these spaces for me more than a decade after his death. The dance floor is empty. In fact, calling it a dance floor doesn't feel right, precisely because there's no one dancing. *Not yet.* The music playing in the space is jumbled so that different moments, genres, and genealogies rub up against each other. Romy's "Strong" (2022) fades into Erasure's "A Little Respect" (1988). *Musical time travel.* Later, YACHT's "I Wanna Fuck You Till You're Dead" (2015) is followed by MUNA's "I Know a Place" (2017). The lyrics of the latter song speak to the longing I feel as I gaze across the room: "It's hard to love with a heart that's hurting / But if you want to go out dancing / I know a place / I know a place we can go."

The sudden shift in rhythmic emphasis and instrumental texture of the bridge of MUNA's "I Know a Place" fills the room. The song feels more open as the bass guitarist and drummer shift into a halftime groove structured by a triplet figure that stretches across the first two beats of the broad phrases. I've written elsewhere about the break into halftime as a rhythmic device used across musical genres to suggest emphasis and collective affinity through temporal structures. In this song, the use of halftime – paired with the corresponding textural and harmonic change – makes it seem like MUNA is sharing a secret with those who are listening closely. Their lyrical address slows and decreases in volume, making the crux of the lyrics all the more powerful: "I know a place where you don't need protection / *even if it's only in my imagination*." QSO's motto and its Janus face echo in my head: "This Space Does Not Exist" / But for one night, we are in a world where it does".

The music becomes more danceable as time passes: Rihanna, then Nicki Minaj, then Whitney Houston. Again, Black musical excellence creates the conditions for people with queer desires to become a temporary and dynamic dancing collective. I take the leap and move rhythmically to the center of the dance floor. Whitney asks from the speakers, seemingly on my behalf, "don'tcha wanna dance / with me boy?" A few people standing against the walls give me tight-lipped grins. The beautiful fella on the other side of the room tries to suppress one of those eye rolls that signals embarrassment but actually reveals amusement – maybe even affection. I lift my arms and, with open hands, gesture to what's happening around us: the lights reflecting from the rotating disco ball, the open and inviting area in the middle of the room, the music that gives rhythms to what I feel and words to what I want. "I wanna dance with somebody / I wanna feel the heat with somebody," Whitney sings, and I think back to Parent's reference to "collective heat" on the dance floor: the way we build warmth and intensity together when we submit ourselves to music and the collective it conjures. People around me are fighting the urge to dance, but I know they won't be able to resist much longer. Dancing can be contagious, especially for those of us who move through the world wanting something more – craving something better.

Halfway through Tove Lo's "Disco Tits" (2017), someone turns up the volume and more people join the dance floor. The song's title refers to the name given to the pectoral muscles of gay men who worked hard at the gym to ready their bodies for the dance floor in the 1970s. The term is camp, which is to say that it can harm or heal depending on how the recipient chooses to take it on. Despite its title, "Disco Tits" is not disco. At certain moments, it gestures toward the genre's sonic markers: a four-on-the-floor beat, syncopated electric guitar that recalls Nile Rogers's playing style in Chic's early music, multiple vocalists in supportive conversation, and lyrical references to feeling high, sweaty, and wild. Within minutes, nearly a dozen people are on the dance floor moving their bodies to the music. Light reflects from the disco ball across bodies, the floor, the walls, and the ceiling. Like the posters on the bar, dancers appear fragmented as we move around and among one another.

I smile and stretch my arms wide as I move to the music, pretending I've got the disco tits – the faggy and flamboyant armor – that Tove Lo sang about moments ago. I turn to see the group that has formed on the dance floor. People look so happy in this moment: three people have their eyes closed and their arms lifted high above their head; someone spins in a circle; another person moves back and forth to the beat of SOPHIE'S "BIPP" (2015). The lyrics blare from the speakers: "Don't pretend, I know that you feel it / try so hard that you can't conceal it / Whatever you're feeling inside / I can make you feel better." One person's eyes open and they catch me entranced by the beauty of this momentary convergence: all of us, music and lights, surrender and desire all bound together in a way that restructures the world. In this brief moment of bliss, everything else fades away.

A few songs later, those of us who stayed until the lights came on are shuffled out the exit. Someone locks the door behind us with a metallic clanging that entombs the night and confirms, with finality, that "This Space Does Not Exist." I look around at the people in the alley who were strangers not long ago but who are now dance floor kin, at least for the moment as we all stumble away from the venue and discuss where we can go next. We share a momentary connection that is built on a desire for more – and the fresh recognition of how good we can feel, together, when we give ourselves fully to music and movement. I try to carry on a conversation as I pull out my phone and open the note that I add jumbled thoughts to whenever I want to try to capture a lesson learned on the dance floor. It's always slightly embarrassing to review the notes in the sober light of the following day – they're half-baked ideas that seemed astonishing and life-changing in the moment but are decidedly less profound in hindsight. Language almost always fails in this type of situation, but at the very least it'll leave a trace I can follow tomorrow to piece tonight back together. I type four words before sliding the phone back in my pocket: "we should be dancing."

References

Ahmed, S. (2006). *Queer Phenomenology*. Durham: Duke University Press.
Ahmed, S. (2017). *Living a Feminist Life*. Durham: Duke University Press.
Aletti, V. (2018). *The Disco Files 1973–78: New York's Underground, Week by Week*. New York: D.A.P.
Allen, J. S. (2009). "For 'the Children' Dancing the Beloved Community." *Souls* 11(3), 311–326.
Allen, J. S. (2021). *There's a Disco Ball between Us: A Theory of Black Gay Life*. Durham: Duke University Press.
Altman, L. K. (1981, July 3). "Rare Cancer Seen in 41 Homosexuals." *New York Times*, A20.
"Anatomy of a Raid." (1968, July). *Los Angeles Advocate*, 6–7.
Atherton Lin, J. (2021). *Gay Bar: Why We Went Out*. London: Granta Books.
Baumann, J. (2019). *The Stonewall Reader*. London: Penguin.
Baur, S. (2008). "'Waltz Me Around Again Willie': Gender, Ideology, and Dance in the Gilded Age." In *Musicological Identities: Essays in Honor of Susan McClary*, edited by S. Baur, R. Knapp, and J. Warwick, 47–52. New York: Routledge.
Braun, K. (1970). "The Dance." *Come Out!* 1(3), 3.
Butler, J. (1993). "Critically Queer." *GLQ: A Journal of Lesbian and Gay Studies*, 1(1), 17–32.
Carroll, T. W. (2015). *Mobilizing New York: AIDS, Antipoverty, and Feminist Activism*. Chapel Hill: University of North Carolina Press.
Carter, D. (2004). *Stonewall: The Riots That Sparked the Gay Revolution*. New York: St. Martin's Griffin.
Castiglia, C., and C. Reed (2011). *If Memory Serves: Gay Men, AIDS, and the Promise of the Queer Past*. Minneapolis: University of Minnesota Press.
Chauncey, G. (1994). *Gay New York: Gender, Urban Culture, and the Making of the Gay Male World, 1890–1940*. New York: Basic Books.
Che, C. (2001). "Avant Garage." *The Advocate*. 54–56.
Chernoff, J. M. (1979). *African Rhythm and African Sensibility: Aesthetics and Social Action in African Musical Idioms*. Chicago: University of Chicago Press.
Crimp, D. (2004). *Melancholia and Moralism: Essays on AIDS and Queer Politics*. Cambridge: MIT Press.
Crimp, D. (2016). *Before Pictures*. Chicago: University of Chicago Press.
Cruz-Malavé, A. (2007). *Queer Latino Testimonio, Keith Haring, and Juanito Xtravaganza: Hard Tails*. New York: Palgrave Macmillan.

Cusick, S. G. (2006). "On a Lesbian Relationship with Music: A Serious Effort Not to Think Straight." In *Queering the Pitch: The New Gay and Lesbian Musicology*, edited by P. Brett, E. Wood, and G. C. Thomas, 69–70. New York: Routledge.

Cvetkovich, A. (2003). *An Archive of Feelings: Trauma, Sexuality, and Lesbian Public Cultures*. Durham: Duke University Press.

Danielsen, A. (2006). *Presence and Pleasure: The Funk Grooves of James Brown and Parliament*. Middletown: Wesleyan University Press.

Dansky, S. F. (1970). "Hey Man." *Come Out!* 1(4), 5.

Delany, S. R. (1999). *Times Square Red, Times Square Blue*. New York: New York University Press.

Delany, S. R. (2004). *The Motion of Light in Water: Sex and Science Fiction Writing in The East Village*. New York: Plume Books.

Delgado, C. F., and J. E. Muñoz. (1997). *Everynight Life: Culture and Dance in Latin/o America*. Durham: Duke University Press.

D'Emilio, J. (1983). "Capitalism and Gay Identity." In *Powers of Desire: The Politics of Sexuality*, edited by A. Snitow, C. Stansell, and S. Thompson, 100–113. New York: Monthly Review Press.

D'Emilio, J. (1998). *Sexual Politics, Sexual Communities: The Making of a Homosexual Minority in the United States, 1940–1970*. Chicago: University of Chicago Press.

D'Emilio, J. (2008, June 18). "Let's Dance!" *Windy City Times*. https://windycitytimes.com/2008/06/18/chicago-gay-history-lets-dance/.

D'Emilio, J. (2014). *In a New Century: Essays on Queer History, Politics, and Community Life*. Madison: University of Wisconsin Press.

Denneny, M. (2023). *On Christopher Street: Life, Sex, and Death After Stonewall*. Chicago: University of Chicago Press.

Desmond, J. C. (1997). *Meaning in Motion: New Cultural Studies of Dance*. Durham: Duke University Press.

Dinshaw, C., L. Edelman, R. A. Ferguson, C. Freccero, E. Freeman, J. Halberstam, A. Jagose, C. Nealon, and N. T. Hoang. (2007). "Theorizing Queer Temporalities: A Roundtable Discussion." *GLQ: A Journal of Lesbian and Gay Studies*, 13(2–3), 177–195.

Dobson, R. (1979). "Dance Liberation." In *Lavender Culture*, edited by K. Jay and A. Young, 171–181. New York: New York University Press.

Dolan, J. (2010). *Utopia in Performance: Finding Hope at the Theater*. Ann Arbor: University of Michigan Press.

Duberman, M. B. (1993). *Stonewall*. New York: Plume Books.

Duggan, L. (2003). *The Twilight of Equality: Neoliberalism, Cultural Politics, and the Attack on Democracy*. Boston: Beacon Press.

Dyer, R. (1979). "In Defence of Disco." *Gay Left*, 8, 21–23.

Echols, A. (2010). *Hot Stuff: Disco and the Remaking of American Culture*. New York: W. W. Norton.

"Editorial." (1968). *Daughter of Bilitis Philadelphia Newsletter*, 1–2.

Eng, D. L. (2010). *The Feeling of Kinship: Queer Liberalism and the Racialization of Intimacy*. Durham: Duke University Press.

Enke, F. (2007). *Finding the Movement: Sexuality, Contested Space, and Feminist Activism*. Durham: Duke University Press.

Faderman, L. (1991). *Odd Girls and Twilight Lovers: A History of Lesbian Life in Twentieth-Century America*. New York: Columbia University Press.

Fikentscher, K. (2000). *"You Better Work!": Underground Dance Music in New York City*. Hanover: Wesleyan University Press.

Garcia-Mispireta, L. M. (2014). "Richard Dyer, 'In Defence of Disco' (1979)." *History of Emotions – Insights into Research*, 1(1), 20–25.

Garcia-Mispireta, L. M. (2023). *Together, Somehow: Music, Affect, and Intimacy on the Dancefloor*. Durham: Duke University Press.

Gay Alliance for Equality Halifax. (1973). "March Newsletter," 2.

Geffen, S. (2020). *Glitter up the Dark: How Pop Music Broke the Binary*. Austin: University of Texas Press.

Goodman, G., G. Lakey, J. Lashof, and E. Thorne. (1983). *No Turning Back: Lesbian and Gay Liberation for the 80s*. New Society Publishers.

Gould, D. B. (2009). *Moving Politics: Emotion and ACT UP's Fight Against AIDS*. Chicago: University of Chicago Press.

Halberstam, J. (2005). *In a Queer Time and Place: Transgender Bodies, Subcultural Lives*. New York: New York University Press.

Highland, J. (1967). "Raid!" *Tangents Magazines*. 4–7.

Hilderbrand, L. (2023). *The Bars Are Ours: Histories and Cultures of Gay Bards in America, 1960 and After*. Durham: Duke University Press.

hhooks, b. (1984). *Feminist Theory: From Margin to Center*. Boston: South End Press.

Jackson, P. (2004). *One of the Boys: Homosexuality in the Military During World War II*. 2nd ed., Montréal: McGill-Queen's University Press.

Jay, K. (1999). *Tales of the Lavender Menace: A Memoir of Liberation*. New York: Basic Books.

Jennex, C. (2020). "Liberation on the Dance Floor: Collective Dance and Queer Politics in Canada." *Journal of Canadian Studies*, 54(2), 415–433.

Johnson, D. K. (2004). *The Lavender Scare: The Cold War Persecution of Gays and Lesbians in the Federal Government*. Chicago: University of Chicago Press.

Johnson, M. P. (1992). "Rapping with a Street Transvestite Revolutionary: An Interview with Marcia Johnson." In *Out of the Closets: Voices of Gay*

Liberation 20th Anniversary Edition, edited by K. Jay, A. Young, and J. D'Emilio, 112–120. New York: New York University Press.

Jones, M. J. (2017). "'Luck, Classic Coke, and the Love of a Good Man': The Politics of Hope and AIDS in Two Songs by Michael Callen." *Women and Music: A Journal of Gender and Culture*, 21(1), 175–198.

Kantrowitz, A. (1977). *Under the Rainbow: Growing Up Gay*. New York: St. Martin's Press.

Katz, P., F. Connor, M. Rubin, B. Apple, J. Maiscott, and V. Russo. (1971). "Intro 475 Now!" *Gay Activist*, 1–2.

Kayal, P. M. (1993). *Bearing Witness: Gay Men's Health Crisis and the Politics of AIDS*. New York: Routledge.

Kooijman, J. (2002). "From Elegance to Extravaganza: The Supremes on The Ed Sullivan Show as a Presentation of Beauty." *Velvet Light Trap*, 1(49), 4–16.

Kooijmann, J. (2005). "Turn the Beat Around: Richard Dyer's 'In Defence of Disco' Revisited." *European Journal of Cultural Studies*, 8(2), 257–266.

LaBelle, B. (2010). *Acoustic Territories: Sound Culture and Everyday Life*. New York: Bloomsbury Publishing.

Lawrence, T. (2004). *Love Saves the Day: A History of American Dance Music Culture, 1970–1979*. Durham: Duke University Press.

Lawrence, T. (2011). "Disco and the Queering of the Dance Floor." *Cultural Studies*, 25(2), 230–243.

Lawrence, T. (2016). *Life and Death on the New York Dance Floor, 1980-1983*. Durham: Duke University Press.

Lawrence, T. (2022). "Epilogue: Decolonising Disco—Counterculture, Postindustrial Creativity, the 1970s Dance Floor and Disco." In *Global Dance Cultures in the 1970s and 1980s: Disco Heterotopias*, edited by F. Pitrolo and M. Zubak, 303–338. London: Palgrave MacMillan.

Levin, J. (1969). "The Gay Anger behind the Riots." *New York Post*, 36.

Lewis, B. (1982). "The Real Gay Epidemic: Panic and Paranoia." *The Body Politic*, 38–40.

Lynch, M. (1989). *These Waves of Dying Friends: Poems*. New York: Contact II Publications.

Lorde, A. (1984). "Age, Race, Class, and Sex: Women Redefining Difference." In *Sister Outsider: Essays and Speeches*. 114–123. Feasterville Trevose: The Crossing Press.

McCaskell, T. (2016). *Queer Progress: From Homophobia to Homonationalism*. Toronto: Between the Lines.

McClary, S. (2007). "Same as It Ever Was: Youth Culture and Music." In *Reading Music: Selected Essays*. New York: Routledge.

Metcalfe, R. (2014, September 19–October 18). *OUT: Queer Looking, Queer Acting Revisited*. The Khyber Centre for the Arts, Halifax.

Munuera, I. L. (2020). "HIV and AIDS Kin: The Discotecture of Paradise Garage." *Thresholds*, (1)48, 133–147.

Muñoz, J.E.M. (1996). "Ephemera as Evidence." *Women & Performance: A Journal of Feminist Theory* 8(2), 5–16.

Muñoz, J. E. M. (2009). *Cruising Utopia: The Then and There of Queer Futurity*. New York: NYU Press.

Muñoz, J. E. M. (2013). "Gimme Gimme This … Gimme Gimme That: Annihilation and Innovation in the Punk Rock Commons." *Social Text* 31(3), 95–110.

Murphy, M. (2018). "Bodies, Technologies, Viruses: Music and Social Immunity in Bio-Pop, New York City, 1980s." PhD diss., University of Pennsylvania.

Nealon, C. (2001). *Foundlings: Lesbian and Gay Historical Emotion before Stonewall*. Durham: Duke University Press.

Negron-Mutaner, Frances. 0000 Dance With Me. In *Gay Latino Studies: A Critical Reader*, edited by M. Hames-Garcia and E. J. Martinez, 311–320. Durham: Duke University Press.

Niebur, L. (2022). *Menergy: San Francisco's Gay Disco Sound*. Oxford: Oxford University Press.

Nyong'o, T. (2008). "I Feel Love: Disco and Its Discontents." *Criticism*, 50(1), 101–112.

Paoletta, M. (2000). "Paradise Regained." *The Advocate*, 54.

Patton, C. (1985). *Sex & Germs: The Politics of AIDS*. Cambridge: South End Press.

Pitrolo, F. and Zubak, M. (2022). *Global Dance Cultures in the 1970s and 1980s: Disco Heterotopias*. New York: Palgrave Macmillan.

Pratt, R. (1990). *Rhythm and Resistance: Explorations in the Political Uses of Popular Music*. Ann Arbor: University of Michigan Press.

Rivera-Servera, R. (2011). "Choreographies of Resistance: Latino Queer Dance and the Utopian Performative." In *Gay Latino Studies: A Critical Reader*, edited by M. Hames-Garcia and E. J. Martinez, 259–280. Durham: Duke University Press.

Rock, J. (1976). "Dykes, Dancing, and Politics." *The Body Politic*, 17.

Roman, D. (2011). "Dance Liberation." In *Gay Latino Studies: A Critical Reader*, edited by M. Hames-Garcia and E. J. Martinez, 286–310. Durham: Duke University Press.

Rose, R. (2019). *Before the Parade: A History of Halifax's Gay, Lesbian, and Bisexual Communities, 1972–1984*. Halifax: Nimbus Publishing Limited.

Rubin, M. (1999). "GAA Must Be Restored to History." *Gay Today*. http://www.gaytoday.com/garchive/viewpoint/071999vi.htm.

Schulman, S. (2012). *The Gentrification of the Mind: Witness to a Lost Imagination*. Berkeley, California: California University Press.

Shank, B. (2014). *The Political Force of Musical Beauty*. Durham: Duke University Press.

Shapiro, P. (2005). *Turn the Beat Around: The Secret History of Disco*. London: Faber and Faber.

Shilts, R. (1987). *And the Band Played On: Politics, People, and the AIDS Epidemic*. New York: St. Martin's Press.

Stein, M. (2019). *The Stonewall Riots: A Documentary History*. New York: New York University Press.

Straw, W. (2014). "How Montréal Became Disco's Second City." https://daily.redbullmusicacademy.com/2014/08/montreal-disco-feature.

Straw, W. (2022). "Montreal, Funkytown: Two Decades of Disco History." In *Global Dance Cultures in the 1970s and 1980s: Disco Heterotopias*, edited by F. Pitrolo and M. Zubak, 29–49. London: Palgrave Macmillan.

Sullivan, M. (2022). *Lesbian Death: Desire and Danger between Feminist and Queer*. University of Minnesota Press.

Teal, D. (1971). "The Gay Militants." *The New York Times*, 57–58.

Thomas, A. W. (1989). "The House the Kids Built: The Gay Black Imprint on American Dance Music." *Out/Look* 5(1), 29–33.

Tobin, K. (1965). "After the Ball." *The Ladder*, pp. 4–5.

VerMeulen, M. (1982). "The Gay Plague." *New York Magazine*, 52–54.

Wagner, A. L. (1997). *Adversaries of Dance: From the Puritans to the Present*. Champaign: University of Illinois Press.

Wakeham, K. (1970). "Lesbian Oppression." *Come Out!* 1(4), 9.

Walser, R. (1995). "Rhythm, Rhyme, and Rhetoric in the Music of Public Enemy." *Ethnomusicology*, 39(2), 193.

Warner, M. (1999). *The Trouble with Normal: Sex, Politics, and the Ethics of Queer Life*. Cambridge: Harvard University Press.

Warwick, J. (2007). *Girl Groups, Girl Culture: Popular Music and Identity in the 1960s*. New York: Routledge.

White, E. (2009). *City Boy*. London: A&C Black.

Woodlawn, H. (1991). *A Low Life in High Heels: The Holly Woodlawn Story*. New York: Harper Perennial.

Acknowledgements

For TBM, my dance floor darling.

This research was made possible by funds provided by the Social Sciences and Humanities Research Council of Canada (SSHRC) and the Faculty of Arts at Toronto Metropolitan University (TMU). There's a weird and wonderful team behind the research that informs this Element. Clorinde Peters is a brilliant development editor and an even better friend. Many whip-smart and hardworking research assistants have supported this project since 2019: Afrah Idrees, Jillian Vandervoort, Norah Stoner, Imani Brown, Cristal Gillette, Rachel Gopal, Isobel Carnegie, Ross Hutchison, and Rachel Bowman. A trio of ancient homosexuals – Ed Jackson, Alan Miller, and Colin Deinhardt – have taught me a great deal about the promise of lesbian and gay liberation politics; I'm lucky to count them among my closest friends. Thank you to the staff and volunteers at The ArQuives: Canada's LGBTQ2+ Archives for keeping queer Canadian stories alive. Many activists, DJs, and dancers have shared their experiences with me; in particular, I would like to thank Rob Stout, Chris Lea, Ron Merko, Philip Share, and Deb Parent. I consider myself incredibly lucky to have landed at TMU's Department of English alongside exceptional and inspiring colleagues. Thank you to many scholarly mentors who gave me more time and energy than I probably deserved: Jacqueline Warwick, Steve Baur, Amber Dean, Christina Baade, and Charity Marsh all taught me to think critically and creatively. José Esteban Muñoz took a chance on me; he still teaches me how and why to dream. No one deserves more credit than Susan Fast, my mentor and friend, who affirmed bizarre research directions and worked diligently to pull out my best work. I can't imagine a better model for how to be a listener, a thinker, and a teacher. Meredith Evans and Maria Murphy have buoyed this research – and this researcher – from the beginning. Thanks to my primary dance crew: Keji, Auggie, Mae, Cohen, Brianna, Alice, John, Sara, Rita, and Ted. And thanks to Tyler Matheson, who fills my everyday with beauty and brilliance; I'm lucky to dream alongside such a creative and courageous thinker. Finally, thank you to the DJs who do the work to stitch together music so I can dance all night in a state of bliss. You create the conditions we need in this moment.

Music and the City

Simon McVeigh
University of London

Simon McVeigh is Professor of Music at Goldsmiths, University of London, and President of the Royal Musical Association. His research focuses on British musical life 1700–1945; and on violin music and performance practices of the period. Books include *Concert Life in London from Mozart to Haydn* (Cambridge) and *The Italian Solo Concerto 1700–1760* (Boydell). Current work centres on London concert life around 1900: a substantial article on the London Symphony Orchestra was published in 2013 and a book exploring London's musical life in the Edwardian era is in preparation for Boydell. He is also co-investigator on the digital concert-programme initiative *InConcert*.

Abigail Wood
University of Haifa

Abigail Wood is Senior Lecturer in Ethnomusicology at the Department of Music, School of Arts, University of Haifa, and past editor of Ethnomusicology Forum. Her research focuses primarily on musical life in contemporary urban spaces, from new musical spaces among religious Jewish women, to the reflection of the Israeli-Palestinian conflict in the contested soundscapes of Jerusalem's Old City.

About the Series

Elements in Music and the City sets urban musical cultures within new global and cross-disciplinary perspectives.

The series aims to open up new ways of thinking about music in an urban context, embracing the widest diversity of music and sound in cities across the world. Breaking down boundaries between historical and contemporary, and between popular and high art, it seeks to illuminate the diverse urban environment in all its exhilarating and vivid complexity. The urban thus becomes a microcosm of a much messier, yet ultimately much richer, conception of the 'music of everyday life'.

Rigorously peer-reviewed and written by leading scholars in their fields, each Element offers authoritative and challenging approaches towards a fast-developing area of music research. Elements in Music and the City will present extended case-studies within a comparative perspective, while developing pioneering new theoretical frameworks for an emerging field.

The series is inherently cross-disciplinary and global in its perspective, as reflected in the wide-ranging multi-national advisory board. It will encourage a similar diversity of approaches, ranging from the historical and ethnomusicological to contemporary popular music and sound studies.

Written in a clear, engaging style without the need for specialist musical knowledge, *Elements in Music and the City* aims to fill the demand for easily accessible, quality texts available for teaching and research. It will be of interest not only to researchers and students in music and related arts, but also to a broad range of readers intrigued by how we might understand music and sound in its social, cultural and political contexts.

Cambridge Elements =

Music and the City

Elements in the Series

Popular Music Heritage, Cultural Justice and the Deindustrialising City
Sarah Baker, Zelmarie Cantillon and Raphaël Nowak

Music from Aleppo during the Syrian War: Displacement and Memory in Hello Psychaleppo's Electro-Tarab
Clara Wenz

Urban Spectacle in Republican Milan: Pubbliche feste at the Turn of the Nineteenth Century
Alessandra Palidda

Background Music Cultures in Finnish Urban Life
Heikki Uimonen, Kaarina Kilpiö and Meri Kytö

Opera in Warsaw: A City of the European Enlightenment
Anna Parkitna

Liberation on the Dance Floor: Popular Music and the Promise of Plurality
Craig Jennex

A full series listing is available at: www.cambridge.org/EMTC

Printed by Integrated Books International,
United States of America